Best Practices: Guidelines for School-Age Programs

Best Practices: Guidelines for School-Age Programs

by Michael S. Ashcraft

Sparrow Media Group, Inc.
Farmington, MN

Best Practices: Guidelines for School-Age Programs

Printed and bound in the United States.
Second printing.
First edition, 2005.

LCCN: 2004117451
ISBN-10: 0-9719304-5-7
ISBN-13: 978-9719304-5-2

Sparrow Media Group
16588 Fieldcrest Avenue
Farmington, MN 55024
952-953-9166
fax: 952-431-3461
info@sparrowmediagroup.com
www.sparrowmediagroup.com

Acknowledgements
My Lord, for directing my path.
My wife, Chelsea, for her wisdom, expertise, love and support.
My school-age care staff and children for adding true meaning to my work.

Table of Contents

The *Best Practices Workbook* contains the full set of best practices and guidelines for school-age programs. The *Workbook* is also published by Sparrow Media Group.

Introduction

"To believe in a child is to believe in the future. Through their aspirations they will save the world. With their combined knowledge, the turbulent sea of hate and injustice will be calmed. They will champion the causes of life's underdogs, forging a society without class discrimination. They will supply humanity with music and beauty as it has never known. They will endure. Towards these ends I pledge my life's work. I will supply the children with tools and knowledge to overcome the obstacles. I will pass on the wisdom of my years and temper it with patience. I shall impact in each child the desire to fulfill his or her dream."
—Henry James, 1843-1916

THE FIELD OF school-age care is sometimes referred to as *after-school* or *out-of-school-time*. These terms refer to an organization or program that provides care to school-age children during their time before and after school, on holidays and summer, at a particular site such as school, community center, or private facility. The term *school-age care* is used intentionally because school-age care is, in and of its own, an important part of the lives of children and families, not something to merely occupy the time of children when they are out of school. School-age care is not less than school.

Children are in school for about six hours per day, five days per week, for 39 weeks per year considering school holidays, in-service days, and vacations, totaling roughly 1170 hours per year. Many children spend an average of 35 hours a week in school-age care, considering before school, after school, and school holidays and vacations, totaling roughly 1820 hours per year. Many children spend the majority of their waking hours in school-age care programs. School-age care programs can have an enormous impact on the education and personal development of children. The quality and practices of these programs determine whether this impact is positive, neutral, or negative.

The purpose of this book is to provide specific practices that will facilitate the positive development of children.

In order for school-age care programs to be beneficial rather than detrimental to the development of children, research-based standards and practices for the environment, relationships, experiences, and policies of these programs must be articulated and implemented. The purpose of this book is to provide school-age care practitioners with a research-based description of the specific practices that will facilitate the positive development of children.

This book is designed to encourage schools and communities to view *quality* school-age care programming as an essential and integral part of enhancing the academic program and educating children. It seeks to demonstrate to families, community members and professionals in allied fields that they must take a leadership role in guiding these programs toward standards of high quality. This book seeks to demonstrate that community resources need to be available for the development of a high quality school-based program. It describes the need for, and benefits of, providing quality school-age care.

The best practices presented in this book are based on school-age care research and theory, including the following works:

- *After-School Programs & the K-8 Principal,* standards for quality school-age child care that were developed by the National Association of Elementary School Principals.
- *Safe and Smart: Making the After-School Hours Work for Kids,* by the U.S. Department of Education, 1998.
- *School-Age Care Environment Rating Scale,* by Harms, Jacobs, and White.
- *The NSACA Standards for Quality School-Age Care,* by the National Institute of Out of School Time
- *Developmentally Appropriate Practice in School-Age Child Care Programs,* by, The National Association for the Education of Young Children.
- *Starting Out Right: Developmental Assets for Children,* the developmental assets research conducted by the Search Institute.
- The theories for school-age care practice of Laurie Ollhoff.

I hope you will find this book useful as you seek to create the most effective care for children.

Mike Ashcraft

In this chapter:

❖ A typical afternoon in a quality school-age care program

Chapter 1
A Typical
Afternoon: A
Case Study

"What the vast majority of American children needs is to stop being pampered, stop being indulged, stop being chauffeured, stop being catered to. In the final analysis it is not what you do for your children but what you have taught them to do for themselves that will make them successful human beings."
—Ann Landers

2:30 P.M.

THE STAFF of the school-age care program arrives at the elementary school at 2:30 P.M. to prepare for the after-school program. There is much to be accomplished before the children are released from school. The activity area, which sometimes serves as a cafeteria and sometimes a gymnasium, must be transformed into an aesthetically pleasing activity space and an enriched learning environment.

Staff members all have roles in preparing the environment. Some of the staff prepare an afternoon snack, covering the tables with tablecloths and placing flower arrangements, napkins, and serving utensils in the center of each table. They bring out two toaster ovens and a crock-pot filled with warming spaghetti sauce. Caregivers fill large bowls with bread sticks, and other bowls with apple and orange halves. They put out pitchers of fruit juice with ice on each table.

Other staff members roll out sections of carpet, move tables around, and arrange furnishings. It's a blur of activity, and the space begins to look less like a "cafenasium" and more like an interesting and inviting program space. An outdoor-type shade canopy and section of carpet define the cozy home-like space, which is then furnished with beanbag chairs, an inflatable couch, a small bookshelf and a CD player with headphones. A child-sized pool table is carried in from an outdoor supply shed, and it is surrounded with cafeteria tables which are then supplied with some of the games from the nearby games cabinet.

An art area is created next to a cabinet filled with accessible art materials. The caregivers bring out science equipment that changes on a regular basis, creating a science table. In the noisiest part of the room, a dramatic play area is created. This week the dramatic play area takes the shape of a pretend grocery story with grocery baskets and a variety of goods; next week it will be a doctor's office. Next to the pretend grocery store is the fine motor manipulatives area which features "card houses" (created from all of the decks of cards that are no longer complete). Like the dramatic play area and the science area, the fine motor area changes each week.

3:00 P.M.

It is 3:00 P.M. The school bell rings and the sounds of children fill the hallways. Some of the school-children meet their parents in the parking lot, while others load themselves onto school buses for the ride home. Other children make their way to the school-age care program.

Within minutes, children begin streaming into the activity area. The sounds of talking and laughing fill the air as caregivers and children greet each other by name, often with accompanying hugs. After hanging their back packs and personal belongings on coat hooks, the children "check-in" with a designated staff person, who greets them by name and records their attendance on a form. Children who are hungry wash their hands, sit, eat, and talk with their friends, some of whom are adult caregivers. They serve themselves snack by toasting their own bread sticks, filling their dip cups with sauce, filling their drink cups with juice and getting some fresh fruit. The children's behavior demonstrates that the children have successfully learned a routine of hand-washing, using serving utensils, and sitting down while they eat, thus making eating time healthy, pleasant, and relaxing.

The sounds of talking and laughing fill the air as caregivers and children greet each other by name, often with accompanying hugs.

Children who are feeling restless ask permission to go outside. They grab hula-hoops, jump ropes, or balls and head for the playground, without eating. Children who are tired or want to visit with their friends or get an early start on their homework, make their way to the quiet home-like space. Others begin playing games, making art, exploring the science and nature area, shopping for groceries, or building card houses. Some of the children check the activity calendar to learn which "enrichment clubs" are scheduled for that day.

3:45 P.M.

At about 3:45, an announcement is made that the weekly *Kids' Council* meeting is about to start. Children who have elected to participate in *Kids' Council* proceed to the school library. A child leads the meeting which today focuses on the pool table and the problem they are experiencing with the younger children not being able to use the table. With little adult facilitation, they decide to make up a sign-up list for the pool table, which allows the younger children a fair share of time for playing pool. When the meeting is over, an announcement is made that Spanish Club and Drama Club are about to begin.

The Drama Club goes to a classroom and begins working on their self-written production of *Alice in Wonderland* which they will be performing at an upcoming parent night. The Spanish Club begins in the library, but later the group walks all over the school practicing Spanish words and naming things that they see along the way.

> *"A child is like a butterfly in the wind, some fly higher than others, but each one flies the best it can. Why compare one against the other? Each one is different, each one is special. Each one is beautiful."*
> *—Unkown*

4:45 P.M.

At about 4:45, the clubs finish their projects and rejoin the rest of the children in the activity space. While they were away, the children in the activity space have initiated a game of *I Spy*. Some of the Spanish and Drama club kids join the *I Spy* game and others sit down and have snack. By 5:00 parents begin to arrive, and a caregiver announces that snack is going to be put away in ten minutes. Ten minutes later the children begin cleaning up their space. The children are accustomed to this routine and cooperate without much adult prompting. By 5:30 the remaining children go back to their self-selected activities and one of the staff gets out a book and reads to the children who want to listen to a story. As parents arrive, staff and families chat about their day, the weather, the upcoming school assembly, among other things. By 6:00 all of the children have departed and the staff, tired but in good spirits, gets ready for their weekly evening staff meeting.

✔ **Try This**

1. Have a homey room arrangement with scatter rugs and bean bag chairs.
2. Hang light weight fabric or mosquito netting to create a stage or quiet place.
3. Have each staff member keep a log of the kids they greet daily; at the end of the week, compare the lists. Is anyone missing?
4. Offer enrichment camps. These camps last a few days with the goal of elementary skill building. Young people can brainstorm the type of camps they would enjoy.
5. Having a voice in the activities and plans is a critical component for children. Consider starting a youth-led council; youth can develop a survey for younger kids and their families regarding activities.

Discussion Questions

1. In what ways is this program a quality program? What are the strengths of this program?
2. What are the potential weaknesses of the program?
3. How does this program compare to your organization? What similarities and differences do you see?
4. What specific skills are the children in this program learning?
5. What is the importance of offering choices after school?

Helpful Readings

Bumgarner, M. (1999). *Working with school-age children.* Columbus, OH: McGraw-Hill.

In this chapter:

❖ Survey the growing need for school-age care programs

❖ School-age care programs help children develop academically and personally

Chapter 2 Research Findings

"Enthusiasm is one of the most powerful engines of success. When you do a thing, do it with all your might. Put your whole soul into it. Stamp it with your own personality. Be active, be energetic, be enthusiastic and faithful, and you will accomplish your objective. Nothing great was ever achieved without enthusiasm."
—Ralph Waldo Emerson

Access to before- and after-school programs has become a priority because of the continuing increase in families who need child care. Welfare reform, aimed at moving recipients into the workforce within a limited timeframe, has contributed to the growing numbers of working parents with child care needs.

Where Are Kids After School?

In 1998, according to the Bureau of Labor Statistics, over 28 million children had two parents or their sole provider working outside the home. In 2001, the Bureau of Labor Statistics found that in 69% of all married-couple families with school-age children, both parents work outside of the home. In 79% of single-mother families and 84% of single-father families with school-age children, the custodial parent works outside of the home.

There are about 8 million children ages 5 to 14 who spend time without adult supervision on a regular basis. This number includes 4 million children between the ages of 5 and 12 and another 4 million youth ages 13 and 14 (Miller, 1999). Exact figures are not available because parents are reluctant to reveal leaving children alone without adult supervision.

For children ages 6 to 9 years old, researchers found that before- and after-school programs and care by relatives are the most commonly reported forms of care while the mother is working (Capizzano, Tout, & Adams, 2000).

During the school year, more than 1 in 10 children regularly spend time alone or with a sibling under 13; and these children spend twice as much time unsupervised in the summer (10 hours a week more on average) compared to the school year (Capizzano, Adelman & Stagner, 2002).

When families are not able to find quality, affordable, accessible care for children, parents often leave their children in poor quality programs, in self-care, or in the care of the television set. On average, American children spend 40 hours a week watching television and playing video games—more hours than they spend in school. Specifically, children in low-income households are estimated to spend 50 percent more time watching television than their more affluent peers. Research indicates that children who watch more television than average are more likely to be obese, read less, play less, and have more stereotyped views of sex roles than their peers; they are also more aggressive and more fearful of violence (Marshall and others, 1997).

We Need After-School Programs!

The perception of declining student academic achievement has motivated parents, schools, and government officials to take a fresh look at the opportunities for learning that exist in the out-of-school time hours. In a 1994 Harris Poll, half of teachers singled out "children who are left on their own after school" as the primary explanation for students' difficulties in class. Both the U.S. Conference of Mayors in 1998 and the National Governors' Association in 1999 listed expanding after-school programs among their top priorities. A 1998 survey conducted by the National Association of Elementary School Principals indicated that two-thirds of principals felt public schools should provide school-based after-school programs.

Ninety percent of parents who say they are not home in the afternoon when their children return from school describe after-school programs as an absolute necessity. For the fifth straight year, 9 out of 10 voters continue to believe that there is a need for some type of organized activity or place where children can go after school every day. Voters most strongly support after-school programs for the potential to keep kids safe and away from abusive behavior (Afterschool Alliance, 2002).

After-School Programs as a Prevention for Delinquency

Young people with nothing to do during their out-of-school hours miss valuable chances for growth and development. The odds are high that youth with nothing positive to do and nowhere to go will find things to do and places to go that negatively influence their development (McLaughlin, 2000). According to an Office of Juvenile Justice and Delinquency Prevention report, juvenile crime triples during the hours immediately after school. Youth are more likely to be victims of violent crime during the after-school hours.

Children and youth who spend one to four hours per week in extracurricular activities are 50 percent less likely to use drugs and one-third less likely to become teen parents (U.S. Department of Education, 2002).

In a survey of 1178 police chiefs, sheriffs, and prosecutors, respondents were asked to rank the impact of several strategies to reduce youth violence and crime. By more than a four to one margin, they chose providing after-school programs for school-age youngsters and more educational child care programs for preschool children rather than hiring more police officers as having the greatest impact in reducing youth violence and crime (Mason-Dixon Polling and Research, 2002).

A 1999 Mott/JC Penny poll found that adults view after-school programs as an effective way of deterring violence by providing children with safe environments, teaching them respect for people different than themselves, providing structured adult supervision, and teaching ways to peacefully resolve conflicts.

Academic Performance and Quality School-Age Care Programs

Quality adult supervision and activities are as important as family income and parents' education in determining a student's academic success. In a 1997 study examining the effects of early self-care in later years, high amounts of self-care were associated with poor behavior adjustment and poor academic performance in the sixth grade (Pettitt, Laird, Bates, and Dodge 1997). A recent report by the Carnegie Corporation confirmed that the quality of child care has an effect on the child's ability to learn (1994). Children in poor quality child care have been found to be delayed in language and reading skills and display more aggression toward other children and adults (Phillips, 1995).

Students participating in California's After School Learning and Safe Neighborhoods Partnerships Program improved their standardized test scores in reading twice as much as students statewide. Participants who attended the after-school program the most showed the largest increases in standardized tests. Program participants also had better school attendance (University of California at Irvine, 2001).

Of the 1,412 students attending the National Save the Children Partners and Collaboratives tutoring/homework assistance programs who were evaluated, 84% maintained high standards or showed improvement in either grades, homework completion, study habits, or other measures of academic success (Aguirre International, 2000).

Another study showed that higher levels of participation in a particular after-school program led to better subsequent school attendance which was related to higher academic achievement on standardized tests of mathematics, reading, and language arts (Huang, Gribbons, Kim, Lee, & Baker, 2000).

In an evaluation of The After-School Corporation, 84% of principals reported that the after-school program had improved the overall effectiveness of the school, student motivation, student attitude toward school, and student attendance (Policy Studies Associates, 2001).

Locklear and others (1994) found that in programs that had received technical assistance to improve quality, classroom teachers reported that the programs helped the children to become more cooperative, handle conflicts better, develop an interest in recreational reading, and earn better grades.

After-School Programs for Children's Personal Development

Over one-third (35%) of the elementary school principals stated that vandalism in the school decreased as a result of the high quality programs in their schools. In 1997, teachers reported that children who experienced positive emotional climates in quality after-school programs exhibited fewer behavior problems in school settings (Pierce, Hamm, Vandell, 1997).

Conversely, students who experienced negative interactions in after-school programs were associated with an increase in poor social skills and behavior problems in school.

Researchers studying participants in Cornell University's Cooperative Extension 4-H Youth Development program found that the length of time youth participate in 4-H was found to have a significant impact on asset development. Longer participation led to higher scores on the developmental asset areas (Rodriguez, Hirschl, Mead, & Goggin, 1999).

Posner and Vandell (1999) found that children in quality after-school programs had better peer relations, emotional adjustment, grades, and conduct in school than their peers in other care arrangements. These children had more learning opportunities, academic and enrichment activities, and spent less time watching television.

After-school programs provide a strong base for nurturing children's literacy development and providing a variety of types of literacy experiences (Spielberger and Halpern, 2002). There is significant research which shows that participation in after-school programs is positively associated with better school attendance, more positive attitude towards school work, higher aspirations for college, finer work habits, better interpersonal skills, reduced drop out rates, higher quality homework completion, less time spent in unhealthy behaviors, and improved grades (Clark, 1988; Hamilton & Klein, 1998; Huang, Gribbons, Kim, Lee, & Baker, 2000; McLaughlin, 2000; Posner & Vandell, 1994, 1999; Schinke, 1999).

Research is strong and consistent that quality school-age care programs increase academic performance, but the reasons for developing quality programs goes far beyond test scores. Focus on improving test scores and you get many children who get higher test scores and many more who are turned off by learning and school. Focus on facilitating positive development and raising better human beings and you will not only get better test scores, you will also get cooperative, self-disciplined, creative, and compassionate students who love learning (Jensen, 2001).

Development of the Whole Child

In *Getting the Most From Afterschool: The Role of Afterschool Programs in a High-Stakes Learning Environment*, the Cross Cities Network states that programs should offer engaging learning opportunities that can attract and sustain the positive participation of all children, including those who may not be achieving to their potential in the classroom. They have found that limiting after-school programs to traditional instructional strategies can "reduce the unique contributions that programs can make to young people's learning and positive development" (Piha and Miller, 2003).

One of the results of the high stakes testing environment within the public schools is the decreased flexibility of schools and teachers to focus on the development of broader social and personal competencies of the kind described in the National Research Council report. A unique opportunity of school-age care programs is the flexibility to focus on the entire breadth of developmental needs of children. In this way, school-age care programs are uniquely positioned to facilitate the positive development of a wide variety of competencies (Piha and Miller, 2003).

School-age care programs increase student engagement in school learning through activities directly linked to school goals as well as through the development of a wide range of skills that children need in order to succeed. School-age care programs enhance classroom learning by providing children with opportunities to practice skills they have learned in the classroom and apply them in real-life situations that have personal meaning. As a number of studies have documented, these program strategies can increase participant's positive attachment to school and school attendance (Piha and Miller, 2003).

According to a two-year study by the National Research Council (2002), young people must acquire personal and social assets in multiple domains if they are to succeed in later years. Schools focus their efforts on building skills in the intellectual domain. School-age care programs have a role to play in supporting these efforts, and ensuring that children develop skills in the social domain. The National Research Council report identifies critical features of settings that appear to successfully facilitate the positive development of children. They also state that the absence of these features can actually impede young people's development. Features include:
• Physical and emotional safety
• Supportive relationships

- Opportunities to belong
- Support for efficacy and mattering
- Opportunities for skill-building

Public awareness of and research in school-age care is increasing. Current research in school-age care is providing important information to consider in terms of differing levels of quality and the effects on the development of children. School-age care is a blossoming profession with a large network of research-based professional and program development resources. While there are no hard and fast rules or formulas for the best school-age care program, the most successful programs offer safe environments staffed by caring, authoritative, competent adults and are a result of collaborative efforts between schools, community-based organizations, and the larger community.

Here's the Point

The best programs incorporate the ideas, cooperation, and support of the larger school-age care community, the community leaders, parents, community-based organizations, business leaders, government agencies, and law enforcement agencies.

Research is clear. Children in high quality after-school programs
- Do better in school
- Learn social skills more efficiently
- Are protected from the detrimental effects of self-care
- Are more engaged in schools and communities

Children in High-Quality School-Age Programs: Summary of Research Findings

- Better school attendance
- Higher achievement on standardized tests of mathematics, reading, and language arts
- Higher scores on developmental asset areas
- More cooperative
- Handle conflicts better
- Read more
- Earn better grades
- Improved motivation and attitude toward school
- Fewer behavior problems
- Better work habits
- Better interpersonal skills
- Reduced drop out rates
- Higher quality homework completion
- Less time spent in unhealthy behaviors
- More self-disciplined, creative, and compassionate

Growing up whole means creating programs that provide balance in a child's day and life. A key to best practices is the quality of adult-child interactions.

✔ Try this:

A literacy rich program can help children gain reading skills without becoming an institutionalized setting. Literacy rich programs mean that children access and engage in reading, writing, and speaking. Try a cooking club where children choose what they want to make, write the grocery list, and then read recipes to make the food. Offer a Model-Making

Club—here the club works together to make the model of the week or month. Model-making requires reading and following directions. Once the model is finished it is hung in spot for all to enjoy. The club atmosphere helps children develop social skills.

During group meeting time try having a phrase like, "What musical instrument do you think best describes your personality?" The children have the opportunity to express themselves and learn about others.

Discussion Questions

1. In what ways are the statistics listed in this chapter affecting your community?
2. Research suggests that after-school care can improve academic performance. Why do you think it is important to focus beyond academic performance to facilitating positive development?
3. What defines a high quality program? Why is it important to define?
4. In what specific ways do quality school-age programs focus on the development of the whole child? What does it mean to focus on the development of the whole child?
5. How does your program incorporate the community as a whole?

Reference Notes

Afterschool Alliance. (2003). Retrieved from: http://www.afterschoolalliance.org/lights_2002/faq.cfm

Aguirre International. (2000). *Save the children web of support initiative annual report 1999-2000.* San Mateo, CA.

Capizzano, J., Adelman, S., & Stagner, M. (2002). *Who's taking care of the kids now that school's out?* Washington, DC: Urban Institute.

Capizzano, J., Tout, K., & Adams, G. (2000). *Child care patterns of school-age children with employed mothers.* Washington, DC: Urban Institute.

Carnegie Corporation. (1994, August). *Starting points: Meeting the needs of our youngest children.* New York: Carnegie Corporation.

Center for Media Education. (1997). *Children and television: Frequently asked questions.* Retrieved from: http://www.cme.org/children/kids_tv/c_ and_t.html

Clark, R. (1988). *Critical factors in why disadvantaged children succeed or fail in school.* New York, NY: Academy for Educational Development.

Clark, R. (2002). *Ten hypotheses about what predicts student achievement for African-American students and all other students: What the research shows.* In W. R. Allen, M. B. Spencer, & C. O'Connor (Eds.), African American Education, 2, (pp. 155-177). New York, NY: Elsevier.

Hamilton, L. S., & Klein, S. P. (1998). *Achievement test score gains among participants in the foundations school-age enrichment program.* Santa Monica, CA: RAND Corp.

Huang, D., Gribbons, B., Kim, K. S., Lee, C., & Baker, E. L. (2000). *A decade of results: The impact of the LA's BEST after school enrichment initiative on subsequent student achievement and performance.* Los Angeles, CA: University of California at Los Angeles, Graduate School of Education & Information Studies, Center for the Study of Evaluation.

Jensen, E. (2001). *Arts with the brain in mind.* San Diego, CA: The Brain Story Inc.

Locklear, E.L., Riley, D., Steinberg, J., Todd, C., Junge, S., & McClain, I. (1994). *Preventing problem behaviors and raising academic performance in North Carolina children: The impacts of school age child care programs supported by the University Extension Service.* Raleigh, NC: North Carolina Cooperative Extension Service.

Marshall, N.L., Coll, C.G., Marx, F., McCartney, K., Keefe, N., & Ruh, J. (1997). After-school time and children's behavioral adjustment. *Merrill-Palmer Quarterly, 43*(3), 497-514.

Mason-Dixon Polling and Research. (2002). *National law enforcement leadership survey.* Columbia, MD: Author. Retrieved from: http://www.fightcrime.org

McLaughlin, M. W. (2000). *Community counts: How youth organizations matter for youth development.* Washington, DC: Public Education Network.

Miller, B. (1999). Unpublished findings. Wellesley, MA: National Institute on Out-of-School Time.

National Association of Elementary School Principals. (1999). *After-school programs and the K-8 principal: Standards for quality school-age child care.* Alexandria, VI: National Association of Elementary School Principals.

National Research Council and Institute of Medicine. (2002). *Community programs to promote youth development. Committee on Community-Level Programs for Youth.* Jacquelynne Eccles and Jennifer A. Gootman, (Eds.), Board on Children, Youth, and Families, Division of Behavioral and Social Sciences and Education. Washington, DC: National Academy Press.

Pettitt, G.S., Laird, R.D., Bates, J.E., & Dodge, K.A. (1997). Patterns of after-school care in middle childhood: risk factors and developmental outcomes. *Merrill-Palmer Quarterly*, 43 (3), 515-538.

Phillips, Deborah, D. (1995, March 1). Testimony before the Senate Committee on Labor and Human Resources.

Pierce, K. M., Hamm, J. V., & Vandell, D. L. (1997). *Experiences in after school care and children's adjustment.* Madison, WI: University of Wisconsin-Madison, Wisconsin Center for Research.

Piha, S. & Miller, B. (2003). *Getting the most from after school: The role of after school programs in a high-stakes learning environment.* Retrieved September 30, 2003 from www.niost.org

Policy Studies Associates. (2001). *Evaluation results from the TASC After-School Program's second year.* Washington, DC: Author.

Posner, J. K., & Vandell, D. L. (1994). Low-income children's after school care: Are there beneficial effects of after school programs? *Child Development, 65,* 440-456.

Posner, J. K., & Vandell, D. L. (1999). After-school activities and the development of low-income urban children: A longitudinal study. *Developmental Psychology, 25,* 868-879.

Rodriquez, E., Hirschl, T. A., Mead, J. P., & Goggin, S. E. (1999). *Understanding the difference 4-H Clubs make in the lives of New York youth: How 4-H contributes to positive youth development.* Ithaca, NY: Cornell University.

Schinke, S. (1999). *Evaluation of Boys and Girls Club of America's educational enhancement program.* Unpublished manuscript.

Spielberger, J., & Halpern, R. (2002). *The role of after-school programs in children's literacy development.* Chicago, IL: University of Chicago, Chapin Hall Center for Children.

United States Department of Education. (2002). *No child left behind: The facts about 21st century learning.* Retrieved from: http://www.nochildleftbehind.gov/start/facts/21centlearn.html

University of California at Irvine, Department of Education. (2001). *Evaluation of California's After School Learning and Safe Neighborhoods Partnerships Program: 1999-2000 Preliminary report.* Irvine, CA: Author.

In this chapter:

❖ Recent research on the brain is reviewed
❖ Applications of brain-compatible learning are
  made for school-age care

Chapter 3 Current Brain Research

"Draw a crazy picture, Write a nutty poem, Sing a mumble-gumble song, Whistle through a comb. Do a loony-goony dance, 'Cross the kitchen floor, Put something silly in the world that ain't been there before."
—Shel Silverstein

IN THE FINAL TWO DECADES of the 20th century the use of brain imaging technology (CAT scans, PET scans & MRIs) and other tools have created an explosion of knowledge in the field of neuroscience. This explosion of knowledge applies to such topics as

- Threat and stress
- Motivation and rewards
- The importance of the arts
- The importance of music
- The importance of playfulness and movement
- Emotions
- Attention
- Mind and body linkages.

These applications have caused paradigm-shaking breakthroughs in the field of child development and education. This chapter is an overview of some of this research.

The application of new brain research to teaching and learning, often called *brain-*

compatible learning, is an exciting discipline. Applying brain-compatible learning to the field of education may motivate both schools and school-age programs to change discipline policies, assessment methods, teaching strategies, budget priorities, environments, use of technology and even the way the profession thinks about curriculum development.

The brain is like the clay of the potter. It can be shaped and formed. We know that through learning and enrichment, the brain will actually change physically (a thicker cortex, more dendritic branching, more growth spines, larger cell bodies, more support cells, more blood supply, more neural networks and more intricate connections between neurons).

We know that the brain learns fastest and easiest in the early school years. We also know that interaction with other learners of different ages and abilities is an asset to brain development. Since school-age care programs have a mixed-age group of elementary-aged children in a non-threatening environment, the programs have a unique opportunity to facilitate brain development. This gives school-age care a great potential to maximize the benefit of enriching the program environment, the relationships and the experiences.

Threat and Stress

One of the things we know about the brain is how it reacts to threat. In a resting, non-threatening state, the *parasympathetic* nervous system controls are fully in gear. This means:

- the blood vessels are dilated
- the heart slows
- the digestive system works
- the blood supply to the internal organs and the brain is plentiful
- the individual is relaxed and alert.
  Therefore, *learning is possible.*

However, when the individual is threatened, the *sympathetic* nervous system kicks into gear, releasing a hormone called *cortisol*, which sends the individual into a state of fight or flight. When this happens,

- digestion is suppressed
- blood vessels narrow
- the blood is taken away from the brain and internal organs and is given to the extremities, so the individual is prepared to fight or run away.

When the sympathetic nervous system is in gear, *the person is unable to learn.* Thus, an important first step to promote learning is to work to eliminate threats for the children: bullying, embarrassment, fear of harsh punishment, poor peer relationships, humiliation, nagging, scolding, lecturing, etc. This makes it possible to learn and creates an environment where brain enrichment will work. Then *and only then* can we work on skill-building and other positive activities!

When an individual experiences threat, learning is inhibited and the individual performs poorly in school—causing more stress, which

> *"Children today are under much greater stresses than were children a generation or two ago, in part because the world is a more dangerous and complicated place to grow up in, and in part because their need to be protected, nurtured, and guided has been neglected."*
> —David Elkind

can cause sickness and reduced health, which causes missed school days, which causes further performance problems, which causes more stress and so on. This positive feedback system amplifies the negative effect of stress and threat and may serve to bring the child into a state of *learned helplessness*, which is extremely difficult to overcome.

Eliminating threat makes it possible to learn, and creates an environment where brain enrichment will work. In the learning environment, caregivers must work to remove stress and threat if they expect children to learn. In human relationships, caregivers must teach children about stress and about how to de-stress themselves through time-management, breathing techniques, useful down time, relationships skills, and peer support. Caregivers must apply the research that shows that periods of rest, game play, dramatic play, exercise, discussion, positive rituals, celebrations, physical activity, stretching, dance, walking and creative writing are effective ways to reduce threat.

> *"The only reward of virtue is virtue; the only way to have a friend is to be one."*
> **—Ralph Waldo Emerson**

Motivation and Rewards

Rewards are effective in teaching a rat to run a maze, but are not effective in teaching a child to engage in pro-social behavior. Short-term behavior changes sometimes result from rewards, but for those changes to last, it is necessary to keep the rewards coming. Educators often utilize token reward programs, often displayed on star charts, to promote desirable behavior. An examination of the research shows this to be an ineffective way to motivate children.

Further, rewards actually lessen the engagement the student feels about the learning activity. Students who are *not* rewarded for desirable behavior actually feel more commitment to the behavior than students who are rewarded for desirable behavior.

Alfred Kohn says

"There are numerous reports of token programs showing behavior change only while contingent token reinforcement is being delivered. Generally, removal of token reinforcement results in decrements in desirable responses and a return to baseline or near-baseline levels of performance...the use of powerful systematic reward procedures to promote increased engagement in target activities may also produce concomitant decreases in task engagement, in situations where neither tangible nor social extrinsic rewards are perceived to be available" (Kohn, 1999, p 38).

Rewards fail to make deep lasting changes because they are aimed at affecting only what children do, and not at what they think and feel. If caregivers want to do nothing more than induce compliance in children, then rewards may be a valid practice. If caregivers want children to be self-disciplined, self-motivated learners, then rewards are worse than useless: they are counterproductive. Children tend to have a deep desire to learn. However, rewards stifle that natural motivation.

Brain research shows us that while external rewards may temporarily increase desired physical responses, they actually decrease desired complex behaviors (Jensen, 1998). Why? Because our brains are novelty seeking, they crave new experiences. Choice and control give children the ability to experience new relationships between actions and consequences, which results in a decrease in aggressive behavior and an increase in productive behavior.

When children experience the positive thinking that results from productive behavior, the brain produces and releases *endorphins* (a natural high). Educators, then, must provide opportunities for children to be involved in productive behavior. When children succeed at something, they experience their own internal reward, which is very effective on the brain and learning. Good learning environments provide children frequent opportunities to make positive choices and experience success.

Motivation must be internalized. Internal rewards maximize intrinsic motivation. Brains are novelty seeking, continually craving new experiences, so educators must provide a variety of experiences as a reward and element of motivation. Choice and control give children the ability to experience new relationships between actions and consequences. This results in a decrease in aggressive behavior and an increase in productive behavior. Therefore, children must be empowered as a reward and element of motivation. Good learning environments provide children frequent opportunities to make positive choices and experience success, so educators must create and maintain a high quality, learning environment as a reward and element of motivation.

Importance of the Arts

Brain research suggests that arts can lay a foundation for academic and career success. Science, mathematics, and language require complex cognitive and creative capacities typical of arts learning. Arts promote the development of valuable human neurobiological systems. The systems they nourish include our integrated sensory, attentional, cognitive, emotional, and motor capacities– the driving forces behind all other learning (Jensen, 2001). A strong arts program increases creativity, concentration, problem solving, self-efficacy, and coordination. Evidence is persuasive that our brain is designed for music and the arts, and that a music and arts education program has positive, measurable, and lasting academic and social benefits.

"The arts are far closer to the core of education than are the more exalted subjects" **—Abraham Maslow**

Making art is a highly cognitive process that involves problem-solving, critical thinking and creative thinking. At Columbia University, a study of more than 2,000 children found that those in an arts curriculum were far superior in creative thinking, self-concept, problem-solving, self-expression, risk taking, and cooperation than those who were not (Burton, Horowitz & Abeles, 1999).

The visual arts (art production, paper and

canvas work, photography, drawing, and painting) improve reading and math scores (Gardiner, 1996). Different types of art will activate different areas of the brain. Studies report strong links between visual learning and improvement in reading and creativity (Eisner, 1998). In a recent study, drawing figures helped improve thinking skills and verbal skills in children with learning disabilities (Jing, Yuan & Liu, 1999).

In a review of 36 studies, James Hanshumacher (1980) concluded that arts education facilitates language development, enhances creativity, boosts reading readiness, helps social development, assists general intellectual achievement, and fosters positive attitudes toward school. By learning and practicing art, the human brain actually rewires itself to make more and stronger connections.

Fine arts programs are known for fostering commitment to task and social skill development. Many students who participate in visual arts programs report gains in self-discipline, work ethic, and teamwork (Jensen, 2001). The neurobiological systems needed for improved grades include quick thinking, mental model development, task sequencing, memory, self-discipline, problem-solving, and persistence. These and other related skills are developed through dramatic arts (Darby and Catterall, 1994, Kay and Subotnik, 1994). The argument that art and music are frills finds no support in brain research (Jensen, 1998). "A child without access to arts is being systematically cut off from most of the ways in which he can experience the world" (Williams, 1977).

Importance of Music

Music's importance to the brain and learning is prevalent in research literature. Music engages many areas of the brain and has multiple far-reaching effects on the mind. Music helps people think by activating and synchronizing neural firing patterns that orchestrate and connect multiple brain sites (Jensen 2001).

"Music is a language that kindles the human spirit, sharpens the mind, fuels the body, and fills the heart."
—Unknown

Students of low socioeconomic status who had been exposed to music scored higher in math than those who did not (Catterall, Chapleay, and Iwanaga, 1999). Music is an arouser of the brain, a carrier of words, and a primer for the brain. In school-age care programs, arousing music can be used during games or clean-up activities. Relaxing music can be used in a quiet home-like area of the program or as background music during reading. Listening to background music can substantially improve reading comprehension, math scores, history scores, and social skills. Singing in school-age care programs not only stimulates the brain, but is correlated with abstract thinking skills, verbal skills, and higher reading scores.

Importance of Playfulness and Movement

Group play, juggling, games and physical activity improve emotional and physical health, cognition, social skills, perceptual-motor skills, creativity, and the love of learning. Play provides many trials and chances to learn, low risk, and time to correct mistakes.

Learning that is active and experiential, involving movement, and arousing positive emotions is more effective than disseminating information in a one-way flow from teacher to learner.

Since movement of the body engages the brain, it is the wise educator's trump card.

Brain development may, in fact, be enhanced by play. The close emotional attunement derived from play is critical to healthy brain development (Gunnar, 1996). One of the single most powerful aspects of play is its ability to bring together the developing areas of the brain.

"Without play— without the child that still lives in all of us, we will always be incomplete. And not only physically, but creatively, intellectually, and spiritually as well." **—George Sheehan**

Implicit learning involves movement. Learning to ride a bike is an example of implicit learning. "A person can absorb more information per day through implicit channels. The length of time that implicit learning lasts is significantly longer than that of explicit learning" (Jensen, 2000, p. 3). Learning in the context of movement provides an opportunity to learn through playful experiences. The emotional "binders" or emotional "seasoning" effects of emotions such as shock, fear, surprise or excitement enhances synaptic connections and provides an additional hook for remembering material.

Learning and practicing skills playfully provides for maximum learning in a non-threatening context. Role-playing scenarios provides for learning without paying a heavy penalty. Intrinsic learning thrives in a playful environment of low threat and high feedback where many chances to learn are inherent as opposed to "seat work" or quizzing where the consequences for failure are high (Jensen, 2000a). A great deal of implicit learning is transmitted via role-modeling, observation, trial and error, experimentation, and peer demonstration (Reber, 1993).

Play, peer games, sports, and "new" games may enhance emotional intelligence by facilitating the encoding and decoding of social signals. Traditional seated homework engages less of the brain. Play is one of the best ways to develop the whole learner. If you want your learners to remember what they are learning, get them involved! Play is one of the most effective strategies for learning and it ought to be an essential part of teaching. This kind of a "break" from academics is actually essential to the learning process.

Emotions

Emotions drive attention and create meaning out of dry facts and information. While the brain is able to set goals, it takes emotion to build the motivation to accomplish those goals. The emotional state of the children and families in the school is directly related to student learning, so caregivers must facilitate the emotional development of the members of the community. Unfortunately, humans often abuse substances to get to an immediate

"Poetry is the spontaneous overflow of powerful feelings; it takes its origin from emotion recollected in tranquility." **—William Wordsworth**

emotional state which may be more productively attained through successes, friendships, celebrations, community service projects, clubs, sports, and building positive relationships with peers and adults. School-age care providers must create a program that provides the environments, relationships, and experiences that promote the nurturing of a positive emotional state.

Attention

Brain research has found that the brain does poorly with a high level of attention over a long period of time. In these situations sustained attention on a lecture can be counterproductive by decreasing the processing of information, decreasing the amount of internal time needed to give meaning to new information, and by decreasing the amount of time available to imprint new information on the brain. Educators who find they have to "reteach" students are usually trying to cram too much information into a small amount of time.

"Getting students' attention and keeping it has been the brass ring in the world of teaching... Generally the brain does poorly at continuous high-level attention."
—Eric Jensen

As many as ten percent of children in elementary school are on Attention Deficit Disorder medication (Jensen, 1998). It is thought that these children are unable to pay attention, when the opposite is actually true. These children are paying attention to everything. They spend a lot of time in a "fight or flight survival mode," paying attention and reacting to every stimulus. This behavior may interfere with learning as often indicated by these students' poor academic performance, which results in more threat and stress, which results in more fight or flight mode behavior, …and the cycle continues.

Children will learn more when spending less than fifteen minutes hearing new information in a mini-lecture and having time to process information through guest speakers, group work, reflection, team projects, individual work, and field trips. Children will learn more when caregivers spend more time with one child and then move to the next child. This creates more small learning intervals while maximizing the amount of efficient teaching by the caregiver. Children learn from other children when caregivers provide experiences that facilitate this learning. Repetition, novelty, active learning strategies, and one-on-one time with a caregiver are highly effective in motivating the brain to give attention to the subject of learning. School-age caregivers must modify their beliefs and expectations in regards to getting and holding the attention of children in light of this research.

Mind and Body Linkages

The brain is a part of our physical body and is affected by intellectual, emotional, and physical stimuli. We must teach with the body as well as with the brain in mind. Whistling while you work, twiddling your thumbs while you wait, tapping your foot while you listen, or doodling while you listen to a lecture are examples of "mind-body" linkages. Children need to be physically active, and need frequent opportunities for physical motion. Children involved in daily physical education experiences show greater academic performance and a better attitude toward school than children who are not (Jensen, 1998).

"We are bound to our bodies like an oyster to its shell."
—Plato

Caregivers should value and participate in the physical education process. Children involved in music and arts develop better thinking and problem solving skills, better language skills and more creativity than children who are not. Quality school-age care programs offer frequent opportunities for these experiences. In a quality school-age care program, caregivers must frequently provide children with a wide range of activities such as: playing physically on the playground; relaxing, sitting, and chatting with friends; participating in drama productions; singing alone or to a group; or eating a snack.

✔ Try This

Process Art Experiences: The purpose of process art is to ignite and engage children in the discovery of the artistic process and the artist with them. Process art is different than product orientated project because process art expose children to mediums and invites them to explore its potential. Process art is expressive, individual and it invites discussion. Our goal is to teach concepts and skills to release the imagination.

Skill Practice Time: when teaching a child a skill or playing a gym game that requires specific skills, start with practice time. When more than one child is practicing at a time, stress and performance anxiety will be reduced.

Observe your program in action. Document the time children are sitting or standing in lines. Is there a balance between movement and being still? Now think of ways to allow for more movement.

Here's the Point

Brain research yields implications for the environment, relationships and experiences which are designed as part of school-age care programming. These implications will be explored in the next chapters through a description of the programming triad of the ERE (Environment, Relationships and Experiences).

Discussion Questions

1. How can school-age programs facilitate positive learning environments?
2. What types of threats can occur to hinder this development?
3. In what specific ways can threats be eliminated in discipline plans?
4. Do you feel there are times when rewards can be used effectively?
5. It was stated that praise and manipulation stifles children's natural desire to learn, why do you think that is?
6. As many schools cut art and music education, how can school-age care provide opportunities?
7. Why is school-age care the optimal place to provide opportunities to make positive choices and experience success?
8. How will this research change the landscape of school-age care and its significance in the lives of children?

Helpful Readings

Jensen, E. (1998). *Teaching with the brain in mind.* Alexandria, VA: Association for Supervision and Curriculum Development.

Sayer-Wiseman, A. (1997). *Making things: The hand book of creative discovery.* Boston, MA: Little, Brown, and Company.

Reference Notes

Burton, J., Horowitz., & Abeles, H. (1999). Learning in and through the arts: Curriculum implications. In E. Fiske (Ed.), *Champions of change: The impact of the arts on learning.*

Catteralll, J., Chapleau, R., & Iwanaga, J. (1999). Involvement in the arts and human development: General involvement and intensive involvement in music and theater arts. In E. Fiske (Ed.) *Champions of change: The impact of the arts on learning.* Washington, DC: The arts Education Partnership and the President's Committee on the Arts and the Humanities.

Darby, J., & Catterall, J. (1994). *The fourth R: The arts and learning.* Teachers College Record, 96(2), 299-328.

Eisner, E. (1998). Does experience in the arts boost academic achievement? *Arts Education,* 51(1), 5-15.

Gardiner, M. (1996). Learning improved by arts training. Scientific Correspondence in *Nature,* 381(580), 284.

Gunnar, M. (1996). *Quality of care and the buffering of stress psychology: Its potential in protecting the developing human brain.* Minneapolis,

MN: University of Minnesota Institute of Child Development Program.

Hanshumacher, J. (1980). The effects of arts education on intellectual and social development: A review of selected research. *Bulletin of the Council for Research in Music Education. 61, 2*: 10-28.

Jensen, E. (1998). *Teaching with the brain in mind.* Alexandria, VA: Association for Supervision and Curriculum Development.

Jensen, E. (2000). *Learning with the body in mind.* San Diego, CA: The Brain Store, Inc.

Jensen, E. (2001). *Arts with the brain in mind.* San Diego, CA: The Brain Story Inc.

Jing, J., Yuan, C., & Liu, J. (1999). Study of human figure drawings in learning disabilities. *Chinese Mental Health Journal*, 13(3), 133-134.

Kay, S., & Subotnik, R. (1994). Talent beyond words: Unveiling spatial, expressive, kinesthetic and musical talent in young children. *Gifted Child Quarterly*, 38, 70-74.

Kohn, A. (1999). *Punished by rewards: The trouble with gold stars, incentive plans, A's, praise, and other bribes.* Boston: Houghton Mifflin Company.

Reber, A. (1993). *Implicit learning and tacit knowledge.* New York: Oxford University Press.

Williams, R. (1977). Why children should draw: The surprising link between art and learning. *Saturday Review*: 11-16.

In this chapter:

❖ Various ways to understand and categorize
school-age care

Chapter 4
Ollhoff
Theories

"Learning and development are interrelated from the child's very first day of life."
—Lev Vygotsky

MUCH OF THE LEADING school-age care theory has come from the work of Laurie Ollhoff. Laurie often discusses school-age care in terms of generations.

The first generation of school-age care considered its purpose to be no more than a place where children could stay while out of school and while their parents were working. The role of the adults in the first generation was to be a baby-sitter or a supervisor of the children. First generation research was concerned with the question of whether child care was good or bad. The only types of training available to adults working in school-age care were a few early childhood and elementary school workshops which might contain a tiny bit of information of which school-age care workers could apply to their field. In first generation school-age care, integration between schools and school-age care was minimal or nonexistent. School personnel wanted school-age care providers to get the children away from them during non-school hours. Many school-age care programs operating today are still operating in the first generation, trying only to maintain safety, meeting the most minimal standards of governmental licensing agencies, if they are even licensed at all.

The second generation of school-age care developed as researchers, having discovered that child care can be either good or bad depending on the quality of the care, now turned the focus of their research toward defining quality child care. The second generation of school-age care considered its purpose to be providing a safe and exciting place for children to be while their parents are working. They developed interesting environments and purchased fun and exciting supplies and equipment. The role of the adults in second-generation school-age care was to be an activity director and supervisor of play. The training available to the adults working in second-generation school-age care included school-age care workshops and technical school classes. In the second generation, integration between schools and school-age care programs was limited to the schools sharing some space with school-age care programs, typically school cafeterias or gymnasiums. To answer the second-generation research question on the definition of school-age care quality, the National School-Age Care Alliance (NSACA) developed The NSACA Standards for Quality School-Age Care.

Laurie Ollhoff states,

"Generation two is the "doing." These programs are safe settings for children and youth to choose the activities that interest them the most. The program environment is child centered, relationships evolve

*between staff and children, child and child, and
staff and parents. The program provides a variety
of experiences that engage the children, expand their
horizons, and challenge their abilities."*

If generation two is characterized by a variety
of challenging and interesting activities in a child-
centered environment, then what remains in terms
of potential improvement? What is generation
three?

The purpose of third generation school-age
care is to be a place for growth, nurturance, and
development of life skills. The role of the adult
working in third generation school-age care is
to be a facilitator of the positive development
of children through healthy interactions. The
question that drives the research in generation
three is what interactions facilitate positive
growth? What actions and practices facilitate
positive developmental outcomes? Professionals
working in third generation school-age care
have accessed theory and research-based degree
programs in the field of school-age care. The
integration between the school (or supervising
agency) and the school-age care provider in third
generation programs goes beyond sharing school
space. Communities designate their own space to
school-age care programs. The personnel of the
school, park, or community and the school-age
care staff work collaboratively on common goals.

Generations theory emphasizes the facilitative
role of the adult and the importance of social
development. The following tools and theories
are products of third generation goals and
philosophies.

The ERE Programming Triad

A basic programming tool of school-age care is to consider the Environment, Relationships and Experiences (ERE) when intentionally designing a school-age care program. We have an influence on children through the Environment we create, the Relationships we develop, and the Experiences we provide for them. Current brain research and school-age care quality research are reflected in this theory.

Environment: School-age care professionals must initially provide an environment, which meets the basic biological needs of children, taking into consideration safety, nutrition, and water. They can then add novelty and stimulation to the environment by creating a variety of areas where children can involve themselves in diverse ways: art, construction, fine motor, manipulatives, quiet conversation, food, science, strategy games, and outdoor play. School-age care professionals can provide novelty and enrich the environment through new colors, posters, child's art, and music.

Relationships: In the area of relationships, school-age care professionals work to establish and encourage realistic boundaries and high expectations for children. High expectations provide children with the appropriate challenges and feedback necessary for brain enrichment. School-age care providers can plan for interactions with fun, caring, authoritative and mature adults, who are experts in child development. They plan for interactions between children of different ages who model responsible behavior and share a sense of community. Challenging, interactive feedback is a key to brain enrichment.

Experiences: In the area of experiences, school-age care professionals can introduce variety and novelty. Novelty in the form of experiential learning is a key to brain enrichment. School-age care professionals need to provide a variety of enriching experiences such as field trips, guest speakers, computers, games, role plays and dramatic play, art activities, and long- and short-term projects.

Interactive and self-generated feedback is a key to brain enrichment. School-age care professionals need to provide a mix of child-directed and adult-directed activities. Research indicates that children can learn to play a musical instrument or speak a new language more easily before the age of ten, so school-age care professionals need to provide enriching experiences like music and language.

Knowing that motor stimulation and activities that require hand-eye coordination stimulate neural growth patterning, school-age care professionals need to provide sports and other novel sources of motor stimulation. Knowing that challenging problem solving helps grow a better brain, they need to involve children in and teach children about creative problem solving. School-age care professionals need to teach children to identify problems, redefine the problems as goals, brainstorm on possible solutions, select and implement solutions and follow through and follow up on the consequences of their actions, knowing that neural growth happens through the process of problem solving, regardless of the solution.

In addition to real life problems children face, they also need to provide problem-solving opportunities through science, math and building projects. The brain is designed for music and art. Knowing music is a brain arouser, a carrier of words and a primer for the brain, they need to incorporate music into the experiences. Knowing how art has such a dramatic, positive, measurable, and long-lasting effect on brain development as well as social development, they need to provide creative and playful art experiences. When planning for experiences, they plan for building a sense of community and for brain enrichment rather than providing activity for the activities' sake. This book reflects the importance of the ERE triad through the emphasis on the indoor and outdoor environment; the relationships between children, between staff, between staff and children, and between the program and the families and community; and the experiences designed through intentional programming.

The Sixteen Principles of Effectiveness

Laurie Ollhoff has identified sixteen principles of effectiveness that when put together with positive environments, healthy relationships, and healthy experiences facilitate positive outcomes—foundations for a healthy life. Ollhoff's sixteen principles of effectiveness practiced by third generation school-age care (SAC) programs are listed below.

1. SAC time is valued as the child's time; their needs and ideas drive the program.

2. SAC programs grow and evolve with kids— children have an ever-changing role and purpose within the program.
3. Intentionality is the key to adult-child programming.
4. SAC programming provides balance in a child's day and life.
5. The role of adults is to facilitate rather than direct.
6. In SAC—movement is life, learning, and living.
7. SAC sites are miniature societies.
8. SAC has access to the appropriate facilities and equipment allowing for flexibility and enrichment in programming.
9. Parents are cherished partners.
10. SAC is the link to education, families, and communities.
11. SAC is a social setting—social skills are taught and practiced.
12. Individual choice and community building are equally important.
13. SAC management and budget are devoted to supporting staff and program standards.
14. Issues of diversity and sensitivity are championed by staff and children.
15. Staff's individual gifts and talents are a celebrated part of the program.
16. The space utilized is kid friendly.

This book reflects all of the Sixteen Principles of Effectiveness.

Five Foundations of Quality

Jim and Laurie Ollhoff introduced the philosophy of the five foundations of quality school-age care through a report entitled *Giving Children their Childhood Back*. This report outlines paradigm shifts in school-age care theory. The theory of the five foundations begins with the understanding that the purpose of school-age care is not babysitting; it is more than providing a safe place for children to be until their parents get off work. Quality school-age care programs provide children with a school-based "extended family." The five foundations of quality school-age care are empowerment, play, community building, self-discipline, and maturation. These foundations are built on the understanding of the purpose of school-age care and of the facilitative role of the adult.

Empowering is a foundation of quality that is a paradigm shift away from "herding." Many in the school-age care profession view themselves as "herders of children" or moving children from one play space to another. After school, they herd children into an area where they take attendance, then they herd children into an area in which to "graze" on graham crackers and Kool-Aid, then they herd them into an area where they all sit quietly and work on their homework, then they herd them into an adult-controlled activity or onto the playground for free play until their parents arrive. Using the foundation of empowerment, school-age care programs allow children, families and staff to have a role in program design. Children plan and follow through with activity choices that have meaning for them, and the adults are empowered to offer activity choices that have meaning for them. Empowering adults ask children how they want to spend their time and empowering administrators ask the adults how they want the program to develop. Adults see themselves as facilitators of children's dreams and ideas. Empowerment creates a sense of ownership in the children and adults. The empowerment foundation is only productive if children and staff are taught the new skills required to manage this power, and it is only productive when it exists along side the other four foundations. Empowerment without playfulness is boring work. Empowerment without community is self-centered. Empowerment without maturity leads to irresponsibility. Empowerment without self-discipline is a lie.

Play is a foundation of quality that is a paradigm shift away from "busy-ness." The adults in our society are very busy and seem to want children to be just as busy. It is no wonder children are suffering from the same stress-related illnesses as busy adults. The loss of childhood is a syndrome described by David Elkind in *The Hurried Child* (1988), and *Ties that Stress* (1994), and by Neil Postman in *The Disappearance of Childhood* (1994). Children these days are being forced to grow up too fast. They need time to play. Play is useful and beneficial, and children need to be encouraged to remember the nature and importance of play and how to use play to "de-stress" and "de-busy" their lives. Play is more than having fun, more than resting; it is the essence of childhood learning. Children who are forced to be busy all day, to be quiet while waiting, to make an art project just like the example a caregiver made, and to walk in single-file lines while in transition are stressed. Stressed children do not learn well, and do not test well.

Adults can facilitate playfulness in a way that will facilitate learning. Playfulness is most effective within the understanding of the facilitative nature of the role of the adult and within the existence of the other four foundations. Play without empowerment is always playing what the caregiver wants to play. Play without community building is "taking my ball and going home when I do not get my way." Play without self-discipline is dangerous at worst and cheating at best.

Community Building is a foundation of quality that is a paradigm shift away from "activity-led" programming. "Activity-led" creates a curriculum that is centered on the activities without attention to purpose, nor to the ethical dimension of community building, thus missing an opportunity to facilitate the social development of the child. Community building must be built into intentional programming in the environment, relationships, and experiences. It involves leadership sharing, teaching caring behaviors, teaching altruism, and teaching empathy. Service projects facilitate the development of these skills, competencies and behaviors.

"If only for half an hour a day, a child should do something serviceable to the community."
—George Bernard Shaw

None of the other foundations can exist without a sense of community and caring. Play without ethical behavior is hedonism, and self-discipline without community building is self-serving.

Maturity is a foundation of quality that is a paradigm shift away from "sophistication." People often exclaim how children are "so much more mature now than in the past." What they actually mean is that children are more sophisticated or precocious. They know so much more about sex, drugs, and the dark side of human behavior or "street smarts." This is sophistication, not maturity. This sophistication comes from the rapid bombardment and exposure to adult information freely accessed through television, the Internet, and developing technology. Children develop maturity through interactions with others under the guidance of mature adults. Adults facilitate children's maturity by helping children to develop the skills needed to process adult information and formulate ethical questions. Only through significant interaction between adults and children can children become more mature. Again, maturity is connected to the other foundations. Unsupervised play without maturity is risky, while empowerment without maturity can be dangerous, and community building simply cannot exist without maturity.

Self-discipline is a foundation of quality that is a paradigm shift away from a "teacher-punished" or adult-controlled philosophy. With self-discipline, we try to teach children the skills so that they can manage their own behavior even when an adult is not watching.

Adults cannot control the behavior of children all the time. Children must learn to control their own behavior. The long-term consequences of over-supervision are children who cannot think and make decisions for themselves. Educators sometimes complain about how children are so irresponsible; in fact they are actually "a-responsible" because they do not understand the concept of responsibility and have not been given a role to fill. To develop self-discipline, children must be given the opportunity to take risks without the fear of failure, and they must learn to try things repeatedly in order to succeed. If we do not give children the skills they need to solve their own problems, we cannot expect them to become independent problem solvers. Self-discipline has a positive effect on self-esteem, teaching children that they are significant and have control over their own lives. It must exist along side of the other foundations. Self-discipline without empowerment is a waste of time. Without play, self-discipline is drudgery. Without community building, self-discipline is pointless, and self-discipline cannot exist without maturity.

> *"If you try to enforce duty only by the sword of the state, you never create a moral being who has any interest in compliance or who feels obligated to do anything other than simply avoid the penalties of law."*
> —**Benjamin Barber**

✔ Try This

Use the information in the ERE section as a way to assess your school-age program.

As a staff, discuss the generational approach to defining the purpose of school-age programs. Look at staff training and parent newsletters for clues to which generation your program is in.

The five foundations can be used to improve program design and adult-child interaction. As you read through the five foundations discuss ways to make a program more empowering, more playful, more community building opportunities, more maturing opportunities, and more self-discipline.

Here's the Point

The Generations is a way to understand the purpose of school-age care. The ERE provides a way to organize our programming. The 16 Principles give us guide marks to see on the way to effective programs. The Five Foundations must exist in the heart and soul of a quality school-age care program.

Discussion Questions

1. In terms of generations, why is it important to strive to move beyond first generation?
2. What specific steps can programs take to move towards third generation?
3. How and why is ERE so crucial to brain development?
4. How does planning for school-age care differ using ERE theory?
5. How is play different from busyness? In what ways can adults facilitate playfulness?
6. In what ways does your program help children with the life skills of critical thinking, problem-solving, and social skills?

Helpful Readings

Elkind, D. (1988). *The hurried child: Growing up too fast too soon.* Reading, MA: Addison-Wesley.

Elkind, D. (1994). *Ties that stress: The new family imbalance.* Cambridge, MA: Harvard University Press.

Ollhoff, J. & Ollhoff, L. (2005, in-press). *Giving children their childhood back.* Eden Prairie, MN: Sparrow Media Group.

Postman, N. (1994). *The disappearance of childhood.* New York, NY: Vintage Books.

In this chapter:

❖ The ERE Programming Triad is divided up in the next chapters; this chapter discusses the best practices of relationships.

Chapter 5
Best Practices for Relationships

*"There are souls in this world which have the gift
of finding joy everywhere and of leaving it behind
them when they go."*
—Frederick William Faber

RELATIONSHIPS ARE IMPORTANT in
the social context of the school and school-age
care community. Relationships between adults,
between children, and between adult and child
must be positive. School-age care providers must
establish and encourage realistic boundaries and
high expectations for children that provide the
appropriate challenge and feedback required for
brain enrichment.

Identity

Research shows that children who develop
a positive identity are more likely to experience
academic achievement, positive peer relationships,
and community service. Children who do not
develop a positive identity are more likely to
engage in a wide variety of negative behaviors
including violence, early sexual behavior, school
behavior concerns and the use of drugs (Leffert,
Benson, & Roehlkepartain, 1997). Positive

identity includes developing a sense of personal empowerment, a sense of purpose, a positive view of personal future and high self-esteem. It is important to provide opportunities to succeed through empowerment by the intentional programming of the adult-child relationships in school-age care programs. Self-esteem is the ability to respect oneself and to think highly or favorably of oneself. It is very important that this ability not be squashed, but nurtured and protected.

Self-esteem, self-worth, self-image, and self-acceptance are all terms used to describe the way people think and feel about themselves—adequate or inadequate, likable or unlikable, lovable or unlovable, valuable or worthless, smart or stupid, good looking or ugly. An adult can squash a child's self-esteem, but cannot alone build a child's esteem. Self-esteem comes from inside people and cannot be developed externally. Self-esteem is an internal asset that is built when children do things that they have a right to be proud of. Staff members facilitate the development of social competencies, decision-making, community responsibility and other skills and abilities that allow children to develop positive images of themselves, their abilities and their personal future.

The way children feel about themselves depends largely on their response to the feedback they have received from the important people in their lives. If these people have helped children to feel significant, empowered, and loved, they will be inclined to have a positive self-image. If people give children a reason to feel inadequate and unneeded, they are apt to find themselves thinking they are a failure and do not have anything positive to offer, so they tend to offer negative behavior. It is important for school-age care staff to provide boundaries and high expectations for children and to value them as important people who have a role in society.

Caregivers must facilitate the internal development of self-esteem in every child, through self-discipline, empowerment, high expectations, reducing threat, and through having a role in the program. When this is done, most discipline problems fail to materialize. The personality of the teacher is a primary factor to building a relationship of trust and respect. There are few skills the teacher may consciously develop to gain the influence that will tend to result in higher self-esteem.

Best Practices for Adult Interactions

- Have a genuine liking for each child in the program.
- Avoid showing favoritism.
- Show sympathy and understanding.
- Be extremely fair in decisions.
- Have a sense of humor.
- Get to know each child.
- Know a child well enough to balance challenges and successes.
- Use of inclusive practices and strong sense of community.

Best Practices for Relationships

The following should be consistently and readily observable in the human relationships of the school-age care program.

- Staff members accept and respect each family's definition of family composition, ethnicity, culture, roles, and relationships.
- Adults know the interests, talents, abilities, cultures, and languages of children in the program.
- Adults respond to each child with respect, acceptance, and comfort, regardless of gender, socioeconomic status, race, ethnicity, ability, religion, or family background.
- Children develop cultural competence, knowledge of and comfort with people of different cultural, racial, or ethnic backgrounds.

Relationships and the 16 Principles of Effectiveness

The 16 Principles of Effectiveness teaches that school-age care time is valued as the child's time, so their needs and ideas drive the program. School-age care programs grow and evolve with kids, so children have an ever-changing role and purpose within the program. School-age care programming provides balance in a child's day and life, balance between resting and active play, and between playfulness and community building. Individual choice and community building are equally important.

The role of adults in school-age care is to facilitate rather than direct.

Best Practices for Adult-Child Relationships

The following should be consistently and readily observable in the relationship between the adult staff and the children in the school-age care program.

- Adults relate to all children in positive ways.
- Adult to child relationships are characterized by mutual respect.
- Adults talk with each child daily.
- Adults respond to children in a warm and supportive manner (i.e. seem relaxed, voices cheerful, frequent smiling).
- Adults encourage children to resolve their own conflicts and give them the vocabulary and strategies to use.
- Adults share with them skills and resources needed to solve problems, without taking control.
- Adults use non-punitive behavior management strategies (i.e. attention given for positive behaviors, redirection, privileges stated).

School-age care providers must intentionally plan for and facilitate interactions between children of different ages who model responsible behavior and share a sense of community. The Principles of Effectiveness teaches that school-age care sites are miniature societies, social settings where social skills are taught and practiced.

Best Practices for Children's Relationships

The following should be consistently and readily observable in the relationships between the children in the school-age care program.

- Children appear relaxed and involved with each other.
- Children show respect for each other.
- Many efforts to promote peer interactions are intentionally planned and facilitated during group times and free times.
- Children act on their convictions and stand up for their beliefs.
- Children attempt to resolve conflicts nonviolently.

In quality school-age care programs parents are cherished partners. School-age care is the link to education, families, and communities.

Best Practices for Relationships with Families

The following should be consistently and readily observable in the relationship between the school-age care staff, parents, and other family members.

- Families are viewed as the primary influence in their children's lives.
- Staff and families treat each other with respect.
- Staff and family members work together to make arrivals and departures between home and child care go smoothly.
- Family members are welcome to support children's learning by participating or volunteering in school-age care activities.
- Staff members make families feel welcome and comfortable.

Best Practices for Relationships with the School or Host Organization

The following should be consistently and readily observable in the relationship between the school and the school-age care provider.

- Program staff and school faculty communicate regularly.
- Program staff and school faculty demonstrate respect for the importance of both school and out-of-school-time experiences in the positive development of the children.
- Program staff and school faculty (typically the program/ site director and the school principal) work together to encourage and facilitate the process of innovation, and to prevent or solve problems.
- The school supports the school-age care providers' need for access to guidance, personnel, space, and use of resources.
- The school supports the after-school program budget through direct and in-kind contributions, including staff, space, utilities, maintenance, administration, materials, and equipment.

The quality of the school-age program is dependent upon the quality of the school-age care staff. Careful consideration and thoughtful preparation must occur when recruiting, nurturing and training a school-age care staff team. In quality programs, school-age care management and budget are devoted to supporting staff and program standards, so staff development must be a priority for school-age care administrators. Administrators must have professional expectations of staff, and staff must act and be treated as professionals and as individuals. Recall, Principle of Effectiveness #14 states that the staff's individual gifts and talents are a celebrated part of the program. All program staff should have opportunities to utilize their gifts and talents through an active role in policy development, program evaluation, program development, and curriculum development.

Best Practices for Staff of the Program

The following should be consistently and readily observable in the relationship between the adult staff of the school-age care program.

- Staff members model positive values, reflect cultural and gender diversity, and are philosophically aligned with the program goals and desired results.
- Staff members cooperate with each other.
- Staff members are respectful of each other.
- Staff members communicate regularly about child-related information.
- Time is set aside for staff communication.

✔ Try This

Play memory games—teaches children to think about and remember things that they learn about the others in their school-age community. Example, "I'm thinking of a person who told us they went on a picnic with their grandparents." The older the group of children the more the children can help come up with memories to quiz each other on.

Keep track of the things children tell you—so you can follow-up with them later.

Teach older children how to interact, lead, and mentor younger children. Example: Big Brother/Big Sister pairings.

Host annual community parties and celebrations; let the children help with picking the themes, decorating, and hosting the event.

Create your own traditions based on the interests of the school-age community—rather than follow traditional holiday celebrations.

Here's the Point

Just because there is a group of children together doesn't make that group a community. Community is developed through intentional attention to relationship development. When programs nurture the relationships skills in the staff, the staff can develop positive relationships with the children and their families.

Abraham Maslow's work taught us that we all need to feel a sense of belonging. It is in human relationships that we find belonging. This sense of belonging will propel children forward in their development and motivation to contribute to a healthy society.

Discussion Questions

1. In what ways does your program embrace diversity?
2. What does facilitate mean? What is the difference between facilitate and direct?
3. What kinds of activities would help to promote positive relationships between children and children, adults and children?
4. Give some examples of how programs promote a sense of community.

5. How might your program improve on the concept of parents as cherished partners?
6. Quality staff members play a vital part in the quality of programs. In what ways do staff members have the opportunity to share their gifts? Why is this important?
7. In examining the importance of the relationship of the school-age care program and the school, how do programs outside the school grounds or with children from a variety of schools establish a relationship?

Helpful Readings

Ollhoff, J. & Ollhoff, L. (2004). *Getting along: Teaching social skills to children and youth*. Eden Prairie, MN: Sparrow Media Group.

Reference Notes

Leffert, N., Benson, P., & Roehlkepartain, J. (1997). *Starting out right: Developmental assets for children*. Minneapolis, MN: Search Institute.

In this chapter:

❖ The ERE Programming Triad is divided up in these chapters; this chapter discusses the best practices of programming for the environment—the physical surroundings

Chapter 6
Best Practices for the Environment

"Raising healthy children is a labor-intensive operation. Contrary to the news from the broader culture, most of what children need, money cannot buy. Children need time and space, attention, affection, guidance and conversation. They need sheltered places where they can be safe as they learn what they need to know to survive."
—Mary Pipher

WHEN PEOPLE WALK into a gymnasium, they behave differently than when they walk into a library. When they walk into a funeral home, they might behave the same as if they walked into a government building, but they might *feel* differently. People walking along a picket fence might run their hands along the top, as if drawn to do so by the pickets. The environment says things to people about the way they should behave and feel. Similarly, the school-age care environment tells children some important things about the way they should behave and feel, so it is important that school-age caregivers provide an environment that encourages desirable behavior. The school-age care space should say, "Play with me!" in a way that clearly defines how to play with it.

Being Kid-Friendly

Special attention must be paid to the school-age care environment. Recall, from the 16 Principles of Effectiveness, that the space utilized in quality school-age care programs must be kid friendly. School-age care providers must first provide an environment, which meets the basic biological needs of children such as safety, nutrition and water.

School-age care providers should then add novelty and stimulation to the environment by creating a variety of areas where children can involve themselves in a variety of ways. The program environment should have a warm, nurturing and encouraging climate, a place where children are challenged in a non-threatening way.

School-age care needs to be a place where all community members feel ownership, a place that they bond with, a place they care about, a place in which they feel pride. The environment must maintain paradoxical tensions by being both:

- community-oriented and playful
- bounded and open
- inviting to the voice of the individual and the voice of the group
- honoring of the little stories of the students and the lessons of the adult
- supportive of solitude and surrounded by the resources of the community

There must be a focus on the great subjects and on the great expectations of the behaviors and attitudes of students. Praise must be provided when deserved; student contributions must be expected and appreciated; staff must exhibit confidence and enthusiasm; and positive interactions between adults and children must be commonplace.

Best Practices for General Environment

For Best Practices, the following should be consistently and readily observable in the overall indoor and outdoor program space.

- The program environment protects and enhances the health of children and youth.
- The indoor and outdoor facilities are clean.
- There are no observable health hazards in the indoor or outdoor program space.
- Systems are in place to protect the children from harm, especially when they move from one place to another or use the rest room.
- Equipment for active play is safe.

Best Practices for Environment and Diversity

- There are a variety of multicultural materials visible that reflect the diversity of people.
- Anti-bias and non-sexist materials are visible that depict diverse people engaged in non-stereotypic roles.
- All aspects of the environment are linguistically, culturally, and developmentally appropriate.
- The program space, the indoor environment, and the outdoor environment are accessible to children with disabilities to allow full inclusion.
- A variety of linguistically, culturally, and age appropriate materials are accessible to children for independent and small group use.

Best Practices in the Indoor Environment

The indoor space needs to be clean and colorful, interesting and inviting, and should reflect the children, their varying ages, cultures, and special interests. It needs to be broken up into different areas, providing a variety of activity choices. It needs to be labeled, clearly communicating what privileges and expectations children have in each area. It needs to be homelike and contain at least one very homelike area.

Planning and preparing the environment can be an activity in which the children can and should be involved. Children can generate some discussion and design suggested floor plans. This will give them the feeling of ownership, while teaching them citizenship and a sense of community. Involving all of the children will help the environment to reflect the group of kids and what they like.

The activity space should be divided up into different areas. One area can contain some Lincoln logs, craft sticks, wood blocks, construction straws or dominoes. This area should display a sign that says something like "Construction Zone" for the kids, and in smaller letters "Manipulatives/Fine Motor Area" for the educators' and parents' understanding.

One area should contain some games with a sign that says "Games" for the kids and "Games of Skill & Strategy" or "Knowledge Building/Science Games" for the educators' and parents' benefit.

Another area can offer arts and crafts supplies for projects that are possible for school-age children to do with little or no assistance from staff (child-directed). The arts and crafts center can be as simple as some tubs full of interesting and varying supplies with no instructions whatsoever, or it can be a project with instructions and all the needed supplies.

In another area, dress up clothes, costumes, props, puppet stages, and imaginative furnishings can be used to create a make believe grocery store, restaurant, classroom, veterinarian office, barbershop, hat store, or camp site. This area should display a sign that reads, "Dramatic Play."

One or more areas in the school-age care space should be designed as soft, cozy homelike areas. Children can design, decorate and personalize their own space. They can make cardboard TV's, or bring in other decorations or furnishings from their own home. Thus, the homelike area will reflect the varying homelike environments in the program community. Adult caregivers must reserve veto power for any inappropriate items. A good homelike area might include: carpet, soft chairs or couches, books, puzzles, soft music, paper and pencils, a table and lamp, blankets, and stuffed animals. Children who want some alone time can use a small tent as a "solo spot."

Another area that must be created is a parent-reception center, parent service center, or "family corner." This is the area where parents will come to sign-out their children. This area should be decorated with the artwork of the children, awards and recognition, and photographs of the children. Important announcements or schedule changes should be posted here, as well as the discipline policy, the rules, the activity schedule, etc. Parent manuals and parent evaluations, as well as information on ways to get involved with the community and with the school-age care program such as events/parenting classes should be available at the family corner at all times. The parent center should be located in an area away from the entrance, close to the quiet, homework, and homelike area, so that parents are drawn into the program, but to a quiet nice homelike place to wait.

A science and nature area can be created in another area. Items can be made accessible for children to investigate: sea shells, animals, plants, seeds, pinecones, photographs of animals/nature, books, bones, prisms, magnets, magnifying glasses, microscope & slides, water things, sensory items to smell, and sensory items to feel.

Another area can feature a special interest place that changes regularly. In this area, any kind of fun item that staff or children can think of, or any special item that interests a staff member or the children currently may be featured. The key here is variety. It is important to have plenty of choices and opportunity to do activities that will interest many different children. Children that are engaged and having fun are less likely to misbehave. Misbehavior is often due to boredom or activity choices that are too difficult, too limiting, or not challenging enough to meet the needs of certain children.

Children need to know what kind of behavior is expected of them; they need a clear picture of their privileges and limits. Contrary to what some people think, children do not misbehave for the sake of misbehaving, but they often test their limits, so it is in the best interest of the mental

health of the school-age care staff to make sure
children understand their limits. The way the
environment is arranged tells children what types
of behaviors are expected in that space. Labeling
each space is another way to help the children
learn their limits. In addition to the labels on
the activity areas, each activity area should have
some posted rules. School-age caregivers should
not assume that because they have discussed the
rules once with the children, they will remember
them—label each space with the specific rules of
that space. Posted rules should be worded in a
positive way—"Walk slowly inside," rather than
"No running."

Best Practices for Indoor Space

*For Best Practices, the following should be consistently and
readily observable in the indoor program space.*

- The space is well maintained.
- There is ample designated space.
- The space is arranged well for a variety of activities: active
  games and sports, creative arts, dramatic play, quiet games,
  enrichment offerings, eating, and socializing.
- The indoor space allows children and youth to take initiative
  and explore their interests.
- Quiet and noisy centers are separated.

Best Practices for the Outdoor Environment

Outdoor space is very important to quality school-age care. It is a place where children learn the social skills they will continue to use for the rest of their lives. They learn conflict resolution strategies that are peaceful or non-peaceful. They learn to live in a community of many children that are diverse in age, culture, religion, gender and temperament. Interpersonal competence, cultural competence, and resistance skills can be built up or torn down on the playground. Children learn about government and global domination by staking out territory, forming alliances, and making treaties. They experience the world of business by trading items like baseball cards and comic books, thus learning about making deals and bargains. The playground is a "kid's world" and it needs to stay that way. They are under constant staff supervision, but they have the opportunity to spread out and call a place "their own," and feel like they are "on their own." Empowering students to feel independence is important for best practices.

Outdoor space is also a place that the school-age care staff members often feel they have the least power to arrange and change. Changing anything about playgrounds is often expensive and time consuming. Playgrounds often need less change than indoor spaces since they were designed for play unlike the many cafeterias, gyms and multipurpose rooms that school-age care programs often utilize. There are a few basics that all playgrounds need to have, and there are some things staff can do to best utilize their outdoor space.

Playgrounds need to be safe, and it is the responsibility of every school-age care staff person to ensure that it is.

- Establish rules: playground equipment is designed to be used in a certain way. Require children to use the equipment in the way it is meant to be used.
- Establish boundaries: allow children to use only the amount of space that the supervising staff can safely supervise. Playgrounds should be fenced. On school sites, where fencing playgrounds is not an option, establishing firm boundaries and supervising those boundaries closely are both important.

Staff can create special interest centers outside too. Sand toys are a great way to facilitate dramatic play outside. Children construct extravagant make believe places, with no material at all, but adding some shovels, buckets, sifters and some cars will help the process along. Allowing children to build forts outside is another way to allow for dramatic play, but the forts must allow for supervision of the children by staff members stationed outside. Water tables and other water activities are great outdoors. Bubble making is a great outdoor interest center, all that is required is a bucket of dish soap and water and some handmade or store bought bubble makers. Plenty of outdoor equipment should be available: playground balls, softball set, footballs, soccer balls, Frisbees, ropes, parachute, etc.

In quality school-age care programs, the program has access to the appropriate facilities and equipment, allowing for flexibility and enrichment in programming. Equipment and materials are important elements to consider in the intentional programming needed to facilitate the positive physical, intellectual and social development of children. School-age providers should have access to school equipment, supplies, and resources, including computer and science labs, libraries, classroom facilities, gyms, and playgrounds.

Best Practices for Outside Environment

For Best Practices, the following should be consistently and readily observable in the outdoor program space/environment.

- The outdoor space meets or exceeds local health and safety codes.
- There is a procedure in place for regularly checking the safety and maintenance of the outdoor play space
- Outdoor space has a variety of surfaces suitable for different types of play (i.e. asphalt and grass)
- Staff members participate in the children's outdoor activities.
- Children can use a variety of outdoor equipment and games for both active and quiet play.

Best Practices for Equipment and Materials in the Environment

The following should be consistently and readily observable in the equipment and materials of the school-age care program.

- Permanent playground equipment is suitable for the sizes and abilities of all children.
- There are enough materials for the number of children in the program.
- There are sufficient materials for three or more children to use most items at one time.
- New materials to extend choices are added periodically in response to children's interests.
- Children are permitted to create and personalize their own private space.

Here's the Point

The physical surroundings where the children are can be bland and uninviting or can be a part of the ways we help children learn and grow. The way the furniture is arranged to the materials that are available—the environment can support our task of facilitating positive development in children.

Discussion Questions

1. What does it mean to focus on 'great subjects and great expectations'?
2. Why does environment play such a vital role in quality programs?
3. How does diversity enhance a child's development?
4. Why do you think it is important to break up space into different areas and provide a variety or choices?
5. What is the purpose of a 'homelike' area?
6. In way does the environment arrangement tell children the types of behaviors that are expected in that space?
7. Why is the staff environment important as well?
8. What are other specific ways to utilize outdoor space?
9. Why are equipment and materials important elements to best practice?

In this chapter:

❖ The ERE Programming Triad is divided up in these chapters; this chapter discusses the best practices of the experiences we provide for children

Chapter 7
Best Practices
for Children's
Experiences

"It has been said that idleness is the parent of mischief,
which is very true; but mischief itself is merely an
attempt to escape from the dreary vacuum of idleness."
—George Borrow

EXPERIENCES INCLUDE activities and projects, curriculum design and implementation. Recall from school-age care theory that intentionality is the key to adult-child programming and that quality school-age care programming provides balance in a child's life. In school-age care, movement is life, learning, and living.

Learning and experiences are practically synonymous. Active, hands-on experiences are critical in the learning process. School-age care providers must use resources to ensure the program focuses on the positive development of the whole child, integrating strategies for physical, intellectual, emotional and social development. Children must also have the opportunity to practice the development of social competencies, as well as opportunities for socializing and practice of social skills.

The Endless Variety of Experiences Adults Can Provide

The school-age care curriculum can emphasize math, science, English, history, theater, physical education, music, journalism, as well as life skills such as problem solving, cooking, earning/saving money, wise consumerism, personal health/ nutrition, and personal safety. School-age care programs provide a unique opportunity for enrichment and educational enhancement.

Possible enrichment areas include:
- communication skills in reading, writing, speaking, spelling and listening,
- math skills in computation,
- application and problem solving,
- scientific inquiry into the natural and physical world, including hands-on applications,
- relationships of people and cultures,
- participation in the arts, visual arts, performing arts, music, dance and drama,
- physical fitness and development of motor skills through sports and physical activity,
- problem solving practice that provides opportunities for decision making and higher-level reasoning skills, study and time management skills to encourage children's responsibility for their own learning
- personal, civic and citizenry skills and the importance of service to others,
- appreciation of and respect for diversity in culture, race, and gender,
- and technological skill development in computer and multi-media technology.

The curriculum of a great school is built into

everything that happens in school and extends into all out-of school-time areas of life and learning. All of the time the child spends in the school should be considered instructional time. Learning takes place at all times, from the time the first child walks in the door until the last child goes home, during lunch, during recess, during evenings and on weekends and school vacations.

School-age care providers must facilitate the development of social competencies such as friendship skills, decision-making, negative peer pressure resistance skills, conflict resolution skills, humor, and knowledge and comfort with people of different backgrounds. School-age care providers must teach positive values such as caring, respect, trustworthiness, social justice, honor, responsibility, restraint, citizenship, service to the community and fairness. For these curriculum areas to be adequately addressed, significant time and effort must be spent throughout the day when children are purposefully put in a mixed-age peer group with enough caring adults who are equipped to facilitate positive social development and human interactions.

The activities are but one component of intentional programming that must be considered. In addition to the environment and the human relationships, the experiences and how the experiences are facilitated must also be considered. Children need an established routine that is consistent yet flexible, a routine that allows for the developmental needs of school-age children. When programming for a quality school-age care program, school-age care practitioners are encouraged to think back to when they were children and remember what did they do right after school?

- Did they go to the refrigerator for a snack?
- Did they get on their bikes and ride around the neighborhood?
- Did they go to the phone or club house to talk with friends?
- Did they go to the couch and rest up for a while?

If school-age caregivers could sit and watch children choose what they want to do right after school, they would notice that children today have the same needs as children did in the past. Some of them go for snacks; some run laps/burn off some energy; some rap with friends, and some go relax and nap. Establishing a routine that meets these needs will improve the overall behavior of any school-age care program.

Chances are that as adults, most people are still primarily snacks, laps, raps or naps kids. School-age care practitioners should reflect on what they prefer to do, as adults, when the work whistle blows. Do they go home and eat, go to the gym and work out, make phone calls, or go to the couch to relax? How would adults feel if when they got off work, someone met them on their way out, took control of their lives and said "Sit down and be quiet while we take attendance and talk to you," and then, "Now you may eat, here's one graham cracker and a cup of red drink," and then, "now it is time for you to do some more work." Adults would not tolerate such unreasonable controls on their "out-of-work time," and school-age caregivers should not be surprised when children resist such controls on their "out-of-school time."

Best Practices in school-age care suggests that school-age caregivers establish a routine that allows kids to choose snacks, laps, raps, or naps as soon as the school bell rings. Children need some time to settle in before beginning the staff-directed activities. Guiding children into appropriate activities of their own choosing is easier than forcing children into activities that they do not select because it does not meet their individual needs. A routine such as this facilitates the development of empowerment.

The routine needs to provide stability without being rigid, so children can know the daily routine and follow it without many reminders. When transition times happen, staff should clearly explain how the transition would happen. Supervision during transition times should be sufficient to ensure safety. Children should not move in large groups or lines or wait a long time for an activity to start. When moving as a group is required children should not be forced to wait in silence. Prior planning to reduce unnecessary waiting results in fewer behavior problems from boredom. Children should not be rushed to finish an activity, and children who finish an activity early should have a new activity choice available. An established routine provides the consistency that children need to anticipate what they need to do and how they need to behave. After establishing a developmentally appropriate routine, it is time to plan the child-directed and staff-directed activities that can be integrated into the established routine.

The time spent goal setting, planning, and

visualizing how the events of the day will happen will have significant pay offs in behavior management. Planning minimizes waiting and down times, allows for organized transition times, ensures variety for the children, and therefore reduces misbehavior that is caused from boredom.

Who Should be Involved in the Planning Process?

The staff. Staff must be involved. Every staff person should be responsible for planning the activities. The more power school-age care staff members have over planning activities, the more ownership they will feel for the program and the more vested they will feel in ensuring the plan is followed. Staff can be divided up into programming teams—one team responsible for the multi-cultural component, one responsible for music and drama, one team responsible for science and nature, one team responsible for the interest centers, one team responsible for 5-7 year olds, 8-10 year olds, and 11-13 year olds.

The children. From the very beginning the needs and interests of the children in a program should be reflected in the planning. Involving the children in the planning builds empowerment and teaches citizenship, responsibility, and respect for the program. It also shows children that staff members care about and value what the children think and feel. It is essential to follow through with the children's ideas, or they will lose faith quickly.

The parents. Parents can also be encouraged to participate in the planning process. They may have some suggestions and strong feelings about activities. They may have some special interests that they will volunteer to come to the center and share, or they may wish to host a field trip to their workplaces. Parents may sit on a parent involvement committee. A quality program assesses the needs and wishes of parents by asking for their input.

The community. Planning should reflect the resources that are available to the school-age care program community. School-age care programs are encouraged to develop a list of local community resources and to make the list available to its staff members. Libraries, parks, state and national monuments, museums, and outdoor recreation areas are great resources for field trips. Local businesses such as restaurants and movie theatres are potential opportunities for collaboration, field trips, and donated items.

Programming Tools

The following are common tools that can be used to stimulate child and staff ideas and enrich the curriculum.

Themes. Activity planning can be based on themes. Themes can be specific for your community or time of the year, such as the Albuquerque Balloon Fiesta, Healthy Kids, Week without Violence, Character Counts, Native American pow wows, the Olympics, or holidays. Here is a list of some other themes that have proven successful: Sports, California, Other Countries/States, Science, Water, Jungle, the Great Outdoors, Animals, Cartoons, the Arts, Wild West, Circus, Time-Travel, Space, the Planet Earth, Mystery, Gold Rush, Sherlock Holmes, the Media, Safety & Emergencies, Pioneers, Inventors, and Heroes.

Clubs. Children like to belong to something and to have control over their own actions. Clubs provide opportunities for both. Allow children to form clubs, to name the clubs, to make club rules, to make club plans, to do club fund-raisers, etc. Clubs based on age allow for some age specific programming and allow staff and children to work on some age specific issues. A special club for older school-agers is especially recommended, since they have special developmental needs for independence, decision making, opportunities to work and play cooperatively in same-age groups, and earning money. They also need to make real things and do things with real meaning. Fitness Clubs, Astronomy Clubs, Movie Production Clubs, Cooking Clubs, Science Clubs, Environmental Clubs, Community Support Clubs, Journalism Clubs, and Drama Clubs have all been successful. A Kids' Council club that solves problems and plans activities is highly recommended!

Put plans in writing. In addition to the promotional activity schedules produced for the parents, each site director should make more specific and detailed written plans. The daily plans should model the daily schedule in the parent manual, but be filled with details. It is advisable for site directors to post this more detailed daily plan at the parent center (on an eraser board), so that parents can see the depth of planning involved. This daily plan should include approximate times, what is given for snack, free time, staff and child directed activities, interest centers, scheduled activities, transition and cleanup times, announcements and discussion/round up. Written plans are an outline and need to be flexible. Offering activities that are interesting and enjoyable to the children is an ultimate necessity, and sometimes plans must be sacrificed for whatever works!

Professional, Intentional Programming

For school-age care practitioners to be considered professionals, they must have a theory base that is grounded in sound research. Professionals must continuously reflect about their theory base and their practices, continuously modifying theory and practice.

Adult caregivers should not just supervise play, nor should they just develop new games and activities, they also must facilitate the positive development of children. School-age practitioners use "intentional programming" when they design and implement the best possible practices in the environment, relationships, experiences and in their program administration.

The research described in this book suggests specific things about the components of the Environment, Relationships, and Experiences

(ERE triad of programming) and program administration which must be considered in school-age care programming. The following practices are products of thoughtful, intentional programming for positive development. School-age care providers who integrate these Best Practices will develop programs that boost student achievement, improve student behavior, and produce healthy school communities.

When planning a school-age care curriculum, include the following vital elements:

- Active play and passive activity choices.
- Opportunities to be creative: art (not packaged projects), drama, dance, music, and play.
- Opportunities for the kids to be involved in the planning and operating of the program.
- Diverse activity choices that reflect on the cultures of children and staff in the program and community.
- Activities designed by older kids and with older kids in mind.
- Opportunities for the program to be involved in helping the community.
- Opportunities for children to develop life skills such as cooking, earning money, etc.
- Opportunities for families to be involved in the school-age care program.
- Long and short-term projects for children to see through to the end.
- Fun, playful activities that children truly love!

Best Practices for Experiences and Diversity

The following should be consistently and readily observable in the program curriculum and spontaneous experiences.

- The staff members understand and embrace cultural differences and regularly plan activities in collaboration with the children and their families that reflect various cultural traditions and celebrations.
- Staff members display non-biased approach to activities (i.e. girls encouraged to participate in carpentry; boys encouraged to participate in cooking).
- Staff members plan activities in collaboration with children and families that broaden the children's cultural awareness (i.e. storytellers and musicians from different cultures visit and perform, holidays of different cultures are celebrated, food from different cultures is prepared).
- Staff members encourage acceptance and understanding of differences (i.e. discourage derogatory remarks, help children understand and empathize with hurt feelings due to prejudicial comments).

Best Practices for the Inclusion of Children with Special Needs

The positive development and education of all students must become the mission of all citizens. School-age care must challenge all students to reach their potential. All students must be educated in school-age care environments, which fully include rather than exclude them. School-age care environments include all co-curricular and extra-curricular programs and activities.

Full inclusion means that all children must be cared for and educated in supported, heterogeneous, age-appropriate, natural, child-focused environments for the purpose of preparing them for full participation in our diverse and integrated society. School-age care must strengthen and support local practices and creative utilization of resources, which address the full inclusion of all children in the school-age care programs and in the community.

Best Practices for Inclusion

The following should be consistently and readily observable in policies and practices of programs in regards to inclusion of children with special needs.

- The school-age care provider accommodates children with special needs by utilizing and developing school and community resources.
- Staff has information from available assessments or may request assessment of child's needs.
- Staff use assessment information about needs of exceptional children and make modifications in environment, program, and schedule so that children can participate in many activities.
- Consultation with professional special educators is available to assist in planning inclusive programs for children with special needs.
- Staff members implement activities and interactions recommended by professional special educators to help children meet identified goals.

Best Practices for Planned and Spontaneous Experiences

The following should be consistently and readily observable in policies and practices of programs in regards to planned and spontaneous experiences.

- Activities reflect the mission of the program and promote the development of all the children and youth in the program.
- Children have a chance to join enrichment activities that promote basic skills and higher-level thinking.
- Regular opportunities to learn new skills and complete long-term projects are provided through intentional programming.
- More experienced children are encouraged to teach others new games.
- Children's interests are taken into consideration when trips are planned.

Best Practices for Behavior Management

The following should be consistently and readily observable in the program.

- Reinforce desirable behavior.
- Clearly state privileges as well as rules.
- Use nonverbal cues.
- Consider redirection or change of activity.
- Clarify consequences of unacceptable behavior.
- Relate the punishment to the offense (logical consequences).

See more about logical consequences, restitution, and a sample behavior management policy in the *Best Practices Workbook*.

Here's the Point

The various experiences we can provide for children are endless. With some intentional thought and planning, we can use activities and experiences to support our task of facilitating positive development in children.

Discussion Questions

1. How does school-age care provide the optimal environment for hands-on learning and development of social skills?
2. What are specific ways that enrichment can be implemented in a hands-on way?
3. What types of programming can facilitate these social competencies?
4. Why is a mixed age group key?
5. Why do you think it is important as a provider to reflect on your own needs?
6. Why is it important that school-age care be different from the traditional teacher-directed school day?
7. How is the concept of restitution different or similar to discipline plans in your program?

In this chapter:

- ❖ Staff qualifications are discussed
- ❖ Administrative best practices can be a critical part of a quality site

Chapter 8
Best Practices for Staffing, Leadership, and Administration

"The ultimate leader is one who is willing to develop people to the point that they eventually surpass him or her in knowledge and ability."
—Fred A. Manske, Jr.

SCHOOL-AGE CAREGIVERS with more years of general education are more likely to engage in social interaction and more professional conversation with other school-age care practitioners and parents, and be more sensitive, less harsh, and more attached to children than those with fewer years of education. Higher quality programs have a higher proportion of teachers with at least a bachelor's degree than lower quality programs. Caregivers who have more training engage in more social interactions, more teaching of language, and more nurturance of children than teachers without such training.

Children in programs with well-trained staff demonstrate longer attention spans, more cooperative and compliant behavior, and more involvement in activities than other children.

Staffing, Leadership, and Administration

Research suggests that staff members who spend more than 15 hours per year of in-service training are more sensitive, less harsh, less detached, and are more likely to provide more appropriate care giving than staff members with less training.

Best Practices for Staff Qualifications

High quality programs will tend to have staff members with more training and education. Here are suggestions for staffing roles and education.

Program directors. Program directors provide for the overall direction of the program. They work collaboratively with stakeholders to develop mission statements, goals, and policies for the program. Program Directors are responsible for program implementation and evaluation, general administration, fiscal management, organizational development, and human resource management.
Program directors must
- hold an associates or bachelor's degree in a related field
- have one year of experience in school-age care
- have six credit hours in child and youth development and program administration;

or
- hold a bachelor's degree in an unrelated field
- have two years of experience
- have twelve credit hours in child and youth development, administration, and other areas related to school-age care programming.

Site directors. Site directors are responsible for the daily operations of the school-age care program site. They supervise the school-age care staff, communicate with families, build relationships with the school staff and faculty, and oversee all program activities. The Site Directors typically lead the Assessing School-Age Care Quality (ASQ) Accreditation Teams (parents, faculty, staff and kids who evaluate the program according to national accreditation standards of quality).

Site Directors must
- hold a bachelor's degree in a related field
- have six months experience
- have six credit hours in child and youth development;

or
- hold a bachelor's degree in an unrelated field
- have one year of experience and nine credit hours in child and youth development or other areas related to school-age care programming;

or
- have two years of college in a related field
- have two years experience
- have nine credit hours in child and youth development.

Senior group leaders. Senior group leaders or assistant directors provide supervision and guidance of children in the program. They supervise and facilitate program planning, communicating with families, supervising support staff and relating to the community. An assistant director fills the role of the site director in the absence of the site director.

Senior Group Leaders must
- hold a bachelor's degree in a related field;

or
- hold a bachelor's degree in an un-related field
- have three months experience
- have six credit hours in child and youth development;

or
- an AA degree (two years of college) in a related field
- six months experience
- six credit hours in child and youth development;

or
- hold an AA degree (two years of college) in a non-related field
- have one year of experience
- have six credit hours in child and youth development or other areas related to school-age care programming.

Group leaders. Group leaders or lead teachers provide supervision and guidance of children in the school-age care program and typically participate in program planning, communicating with families, supervising support staff and relating to the community.

Group Leaders or lead teachers must
- have a bachelor's degree in a related field;

or
- hold a bachelor's degree in an unrelated field
- have three months of experience
- have three credit hours in child and youth development;

or
- have two years of college
- have nine months of experience

- have three credit hours in child and youth development;

or

- hold a high school diploma
- have 18 months of experience
- have six credit hours in child and youth development or areas related to school-age care programming.

Best Practices for Staffing Practices

The following should be consistently and readily observable in the program.

- Enough qualified staff members are in place to meet all levels of responsibility.
- Qualified staff members are hired in all areas: to administer the program, to oversee its daily operations, and to supervise children.
- The administration provides all new staff with an in-depth pre-service orientation to the program and provides them with on-going support and supervision.
- The administration strives to pay staff commensurate with their training and experience.
- Staff members are given paid preparation time.

Child-Staff Ratio and Group Size

Small child-staff ratios and group sizes permit the staff to meet the needs of children and youth. Fewer children per adult and small group size result in: less stress for children and teachers, higher frequencies of positive child and teacher behaviors, greater gains in positive development of children, more frequent and longer child-adult

interactions, better curriculum, and more positive
social play and peer interactions.

Best Practices for Child-Staff Ratio and Group Size

The following should be consistently and readily observable in regards to the child-staff ratio and group size.

- Child-staff ratios vary according to the ages and abilities of children. For groups of children age 6 and older, the ratio is between 10:1 and 15:1. For groups that include children under the age of 6, the ratio is between 8:1 and 12:1.
- When divided into small groups, group sizes typically stay less than fifteen children accompanied by at least one adult caregiver.
- Child-staff ratios and group sizes vary according to the type and complexity of the activity, but group sizes do not exceed thirty.
- There is a plan to provide adequate staff coverage in case of emergencies.
- Substitute staff members are used to maintain ratios when regular staff members are absent.

Training and Professional Development

The following should be the standard in terms of training and professional development:

- Written staff responsibilities to children, families, and the program and personnel policies are reviewed with each staff member.
- Staff members have received the recommended type and amount of pre-service preparation. They meet the

requirements that are specific to school-age child care and relevant to their particular jobs.

- Staff members receive training in effectively working with families and meeting the needs of children in ways that promote the child's development.
- A listing of workshops, seminars, and other staff development opportunities offered by local trainers, community colleges, churches and community organizations is displayed prominently and staff members are encouraged and paid to attend.
- Regularly scheduled staff meetings include staff development activities.

Assessment of Programs

Assessment of children and programs is an on-going and ever changing process that is shared with the whole program community. Multiple indicators and sources of information must be used to properly assess the school-age care program. All program staff, family members, and children provide evaluative feedback that is considered in program assessment. External evaluations such as the State Department of Education's Standards for Excellence, the School-Age Care Environment Rating Scale, and or the National School-Age Care Alliance's Standards for Quality School-Age Care should be used for program assessment.

Administrators must assist with ongoing evaluation. They aim for improvement in all areas of the program. All program staff participate in a process of continuous program evaluation and improvement.

The program can use the Advancing and Recognizing School-Age Care Quality (ARQ) tool produced by the National School-Age Care Alliance (NSACA) for program assessment and program quality improvement.

Best Practices for Family and Community Collaboration

The following should be consistently and readily observable in the collaborative practices between families, the community, and the school-age care program.

- Community members are invited to share their special talents and expertise with children in the school-age care program.
- The program builds links to the community.
- Staff members provide information about community resources to meet the needs of children and their families.
- The staff members plan activities to help children get to know the larger community.
- The program develops a list of community resources. The staff members draw from these resources to expand program offerings.

Administration of School-Age Care Programs

In quality school-age care programs the management and budget are devoted to supporting staff and program standards. Everything about the management and budget should be driven by the goal of supporting staff and supporting standards that are in the best interests of staff and children.

Best Practices for the Administration of School-Age Care Programs

The following should be consistently and readily observable in the administrative policies and practices in the school-age care program.

- The administration is knowledgeable about how children grow, develop, and learn.
- The administration assumes leadership in developing and articulating the program's philosophy, mission, and goals.
- The administration engages in on-going professional development.
- The program hours of operation are based on families' needs.
- The school-age care administration implements a plan for improving staff recruitment and retention and for providing adequate financial compensation and benefits.

The Role of the School

The actual role schools play, in regards to the school-age care programs housed within their walls, varies greatly. In some cases the elementary school acts as the school-age care provider. The school board or another school committee is the governing entity. The school recruits and supervises the school-age caregivers, administers the fiscal operations, and develops operational goals for the program. In other cases the school shares responsibility of the administration of the school-age care program with a school-based committee, parent-teacher organization, informal group of school faculty, or community based organization. In other cases, a community-based organization is solely responsible for the governance and administration of the school-age care program. In all cases, the school can provide leadership in establishing communication, cooperation, collaboration, and participation among families, school staff and faculty, and school-age caregivers.

The elementary school principal is the key in motivating staff to build connections between school-day and out-of-school time experiences. The principal is also vital in ensuring that the school space, administrative support, custodial support, and other school resources are available to the school-age care program. Along with the principal, the faculty and support staff members should be active participants in the out-of-school time programs. The principal is the key in determining in what ways the school and its staff are most equipped and most prepared to support and enhance the school-age care programs.

While schools can easily provide space, accessibility, transportation, custodial staff, administrative support, resources, and liability protection, additional responsibilities may strain existing staff functions and diminish the effectiveness of classroom learning because of other educational priorities. For this reason, a well-established, community-based organization, dedicated to high quality school-age care, may offer schools the following: experienced and educated school-age care staff; expertise in handling time and resource consuming details; an existing system of school-age care management;

and ongoing funding and administrative resource (National Association of Elementary School Principals, 1999).

The school has a vital role to play regardless of how the school-age care program is managed. The school typically has well-established relationships with the community, government agencies, religious groups, civic organizations, and other school personnel; thus the school is in an excellent position to serve as a gateway between the school-age care program and the greater community. The school can assist with the community's acceptance of the school-age care program through communication. Principals promote a team approach to quality school-age care programming by encouraging teachers to share classroom space, custodians to assist in the maintenance of the program space, cafeteria managers to ensure accessibility of space and equipment, school bus drivers to take the children home, and school secretaries to take messages and give out school-age care information. The school can help meet the school-age care providers' need for access to phones, administrative assistance, library, gymnasium, art rooms, computer rooms and other classrooms. This need is often a source of tension between school day and out-of-school-time staff, but the principal can facilitate acceptance by working with both groups to establish clear agreements and solving problems collaboratively.

Regular meetings are necessary to establish protocol for sharing space, develop consistent policies and procedures, design curriculum development goals, and forge linkages between school and school-age care provider. Schools that contract with community-based organizations should require that certain standards are met and that the program is regularly assessed and evaluated. All school-based programs should be licensed by their local child care licensing authority and whenever possible exceed minimal licensing standards.

Here's the Point

Research suggests that better trained staff provide more quality care. Since the most important factor in a quality site is the staff, it pays big dividends to invest in the training of the staff.

Discussion Questions

1. How does education support the profession?
2. Why is continual professional development important?
3. In what ways does family and community collaboration improve program quality?
4. What might be some ways change can begin within your program?
5. In what ways does assessment improve quality? What types of assessment have you used in the program?

Reference Notes

National Association of Elementary School Principals. (1999). *After-school programs and the K-8 principal: Standards for quality school-age child care.* Alexandria, VI: National Association of Elementary School Principals.

National School-Age Care Alliance. (1998). *Advancing and recognizing quality: Guide to NSACA program accreditation.* Boston, MA: National School-Age Care Alliance.

Chapter 9
Conclusion

"If you want to move people, it has to be toward a vision that's positive for them, that taps important values, that gets them something they desire, and it has to be presented in a compelling way that they feel inspired to follow."
—Martin Luther King Jr.

QUALITY SCHOOL-AGE CARE is more than a safe place for kids to be while their parents are working, and it is more than a fun place to be. It is one of the few times in a child's day which provides the opportunity to interact positively with children of different ages. It is perhaps the only time in a day that caring adults, who have the time to give significant one-on-one attention to children, are available. We have the unique ability to teach the social skills that are essential in youth development, delinquency prevention, and the development of the future citizens of this country. We join, in true partnership, with the family and the school in the role of participating in the positive development and education of our children.

The vision for school-age care is ideological, but possible. It is challenging, but realistic. It is not a wishful fantasy, but an attainable picture of our future. It is the result of accomplishing our goals and our mission. The vision is that of a wonderful place filled with an extended family in true partnership with schools and families. It is a community that nurtures and truly cares for children, staff, and families. It is a mini-society that challenges children, staff, and families to be their best. It is a place where children, staff, and families learn and develop life skills. It is a place that facilitates or makes easier the positive development and education of children. The vision of school-age care is to see healthier children, healthier families, and a healthier community.

An essential element of being a professional is having a theory base. Professional school-age care practitioners must constantly learn and develop their theory base, revising their day-to-day practices based on new learning. They must be lifelong learners and critically reflective practitioners. Research in school-age care is continuous and on-going. This new research will shed new light on school-age care. Best practices based on this new research will change to reflect new knowledge. Change is the only constant. It is part of our culture, part of our lives. School-age care practitioners are challenged to anticipate and embrace change and cautioned to use phrases like, "the way things are done around here" only with serious consideration of their core values, and of what is in the best interest of the children and families in our community.

> *"Leadership and learning are indispensable to each other."*
> *—John F. Kennedy*

Glossary

Abuse: means any act or failure to act, performed intentionally, knowingly or recklessly that causes or is likely to cause harm to a child, including: physical contact that harms or is likely to harm a child; inappropriate use of physical restraint, isolation, medication, or other means that harms or is likely to harm a child; an unlawful act, a threat or menacing conduct directed toward a child that results and/or might be expected to result in fear or emotional or mental distress to a child.

Activity Area means space for children's activities where related equipment and materials are accessible to the children.

Adult means a person who has a chronological age of 18 years or older.

Capacity means the maximum number of children a program can provide care for at any one time, based on the number of staff and the amount of appropriate activity areas, indoor space, and outdoor space.

Caregiver means an adult who directly cares for, serves, and supervises children in a school-age care program. Caregivers (staff members) who work directly with children and who are counted in the child-staff ratios must be eighteen (18) years of age or older.

Child means a person who is under the chronological age of eighteen (18) years.

Child-Staff Ratio means the ratio of the number of child program participants to the number of adult caregivers present. For example the minimum child-staff ratio is no more than 15 children per 1 adult caregiver. 15:1.

Children & Youth mean any people under the age of 18 years.

Courses in School-Age Care Programming includes courses in topic areas such as supervision, health and safety, developmentally appropriate practices, guidance, community service and service learning, working with families, community outreach, and planning activities.

Community means the residents, businesses, and public use areas in the general area of the population of the program.

Credit Hours means credit hours for post-secondary coursework. Each credit represents approximately 15 hours of participation in a course.

Culture encompasses all socially transmitted behavior patterns, arts, beliefs, institutions, and all other products of human work and thought typical of a population or community at a given time; a process that consists of a set of rules or expectations for the behavior of group members that are passed on from one generation to the next.

Developmentally Appropriate Practices means those practices which result from decisions made about the well being and education of children based on what is known about child development and learning, what is known about each individual child, and what is known about the cultural contexts in which the children live.

Discipline means teaching and guidance, which fosters the child's ability to become self-disciplined. Disciplinary measures will be consistent and developmentally appropriate.

Experience means related experience, or work with school-age children in a recreational, fine arts, camping or academic setting, including but not limited to: licensed or registered family school-age care programs, licensed center-based school-age education and development programs, elementary school classrooms and family support programs. One year's experience means full-time (2080 hours of work).

Family means the immediate group of people with whom the child lives.

Group Leader means an entry-level adult staff member whose primary function is to supervise, interact with, and provide guidance to the child program participants.

Group Size means the size of a group of children when they are separated into special activity groups, age-specific groups, or groups who transition at the same time.

Guardian see Parent.

Indoor Space/Indoor Environment means the indoor activity areas that the children use, indoor working areas utilized by the staff, bathrooms, and indoor public and traffic areas.

Intentional Programming means the thoughtful design of program environment, human relationships, and program experiences.

Neglect means the failure to provide the proper care and common necessities including but not limited to: food, shelter, a safe environment, education, and healthcare that may result in harm to the child.

Outdoor Space or Environment means the outdoor activity areas that the children use, parking lots, and outdoor public or traffic areas.

Parent for the sake of efficiency, in this document the word "parent" means parent or parents, guardian or guardians, grandparent, foster-parent, or other adult who has legal custody, responsibility and authority over the child.

Premises means all parts of the buildings, grounds, and equipment of a school-age care program.

Program Director means the person responsible for planning or implementing the care of children in one or more school-age care programs. This includes but is not limited to building relationships with parents, keeping appropriate records, overseeing fiscal management, observing and evaluating the child's development, supervising staff members and volunteers, and working cooperatively with the site director and other staff members toward achieving program goals and objectives. The program director may develop missions, goals, and policies of the program.

Program Space means the indoor and outdoor space of the program, including all space utilized by children, staff or families.

Physical Punishment means the touching of a child's body with the intent of inducing pain. This includes but is not limited to pinching, shaking, spanking, hair, or ear pulling.

Related Field (to school-age care) includes majors in early childhood education, youth studies, child development, recreation, family social sciences, and elementary education.

School-Age Care means an organization or program that provides care to school-age children (ages 4-14) during their out-of-school time, at a particular site such as school, community center, or private facility.

School-Age Care Provider means the school, school-based, or community based organization, which is primarily or partially responsible for the administration of the school-age care, enrichment, recreation, or before- and/or after-school program.

Senior Group Leader means a person who typically provides supervision and guidance to children, and leadership to fellow staff members in areas such as program planning, and staff supervision and development.

Site Director means the person at the site having responsibility for program administration and the day-to-day supervision of a school age program. The Site Director typically communicates with families, builds relationships with the host community, and oversees all program activities.

Supervision means the direct observation and guidance of children at all times and requires being physically present with them. The only exception is school-age children who will have privacy in the use of bathrooms.

Transitions means the times when children are moving from one type of activity to another such as transitioning from school to after-school, from child directed activity to adult directed activity, or from child selected activity to a field trip.

Index

A

Academic performance, 25, 28, 32, 34, 51-52

Arts, 26, 31, 39, 45-47, 52, 87, 89, 91, 100, 106, 131-133

Assessment, 40, 110, 121-122, 126

C

Communities, 10, 30, 59, 63, 78, 108

Community Based Organizations

Competencies, 28-29, 65, 74, 99, 101, 112

E

Elkind, David, 41, 65

Emotional development, 49

Empowerment, 64-68, 74-75, 103-104

Environment, 10-11, 13, 24, 28, 30, 40-42, 44-45, 49-50, 53, 66, 84-88, 91-92, 94-96, 101, 106-107, 109-110, 112, 121, 133

ERE theory, 60-62, 68-69

F

Facilitate-facilitator, 10, 29, 40, 46, 49, 51, 53, 59, 62-63, 65-67, 74-75, 77, 93-94, 101, 103, 107, 125, 129

G

Generation Theory, 57-59, 62, 68-69

I

Intentional programming, 62, 66, 74, 94, 101, 107-108, 111, 133

Internal asset, 74

L

Learned helplessness, 42

Literacy, 27, 31, 36

M

Maslow, Abraham, 81

Motivation, 26, 31, 39, 42-45, 49, 81

Music, 9, 32, 39, 45-47, 52-53, 60-62, 89

N

Neuroscience, 39

Best Practices Index

About the Author

Mike Ashcraft is the CEO of Children's Choice Child Care Services in Albuquerque, New Mexico. He and his wife Chelsea are the co-founders and CEOs of the organization which provides school-age care programs in Albuquerque and staff training and technical assistance all across the country. They both provide training in the areas of Afterschool Environments, Curriculum, Behavior Management, Social Development, Brain Development, Leadership, and a course on Brain-Compatible Staff Training. Mike holds a Master of Arts Degree in Education with an Emphasis in School-Age Care from Concordia University. He is a doctoral candidate with Nova Southeastern University in Organizational Leadership with an Emphasis in Not-For-Profit Organizations. He has more than 18 years of experience in school-age care. He is an Accreditation Endorser for the National Afterschool Alliance. He is an experienced trainer of trainers in the field of School-Age Care. He has served as a training and technical service contractor and a professional writing contractor for the New Mexico State Department of Education. He serves as an adjunct professor on the faculty of Concordia University, teaching college courses in school-age care programming. He is certified as an Advanced Quality Advisor from the National Institute on Out of School Time. He is the current President of the New Mexico School-Age Care Alliance and the current Secretary of the New Mexico Association for the Education of Young Children. Mike's academic interests include science, leadership, brain-compatible learning, and adult learning. Mike and Chelsea have one incredible daughter, Madison, and they are expecting another child in May of 2005. For fun, Mike reads, skis, gardens, listens to music, and plays with his daughter. He can be reached at ashcraft@childrens-choice.org.